JB JOSSEY-BASS™
A Wiley Brand

Making the Ask

149 Tips for Soliciting Major Gifts

Scott C. Stevenson, Editor

WILEY

978-1-118-69307-0   ISBN

978-1-118-70424-0   ISBN (online)

Making the Ask

149 Tips for Soliciting Major Gifts

Published by

Stevenson, Inc.

P.O. Box 4528 • Sioux City, Iowa • 51104
Phone 712.239.3010 • Fax 712.239.2166
www.stevensoninc.com

TABLE OF CONTENTS

TABLE OF CONTENTS

Making the Ask: 149 Tips for Soliciting Major Gifts.
Edited by Scott C. Stevenson.
© 2009 Stevenson, Inc. Published 2009 by Stevenson, Inc.

1. Selection and Preparation Are Key to First-time Ask

When preparing for your first major gift ask, be sure to start with an individual close to your organization, says Linda Haley, director of fund development services, Zielinski Companies (St. Louis, MO). "Take your time to build a good relationship," she says. "Learn as much as you can before your first meeting. You're not in the business of hurrying to get major gifts. You want the donor to feel great about making a gift."

Once you choose your major gift prospect, Haley suggests following these pre-ask steps:

1. Identify and visit with someone within your organization who knows your prospect well. Have a pre-meeting to determine salient points that should be made. Listen carefully and identify questions your prospect may have about your organization.

2. Work to build a relationship with the prospect around the organization and its mission, not just with one person involved in the organization.

3. Determine the prospect's level of interest in your organization's mission. If it is low, you may need to spend more time educating and inspiring your prospective donor.

4. Determine what most excited your prospect during the meeting and identify a logical, natural next step that builds on the prospect's enthusiasm.

5. On your next visit, begin talking about how the prospect can help. You want the conversation to become an exchange of ideas. You will be nervous when you make your first ask, but you should feel confident. If you don't feel good about asking for a gift, it's not the right time. When the donor feels good and you feel good, the outcome will be positive for the organization.

Between cultivation steps, says Haley, make sure you are making a touch with the prospect every month. "The touch should be something personal and meaningful that keeps you in contact with your prospect. For example, a phone call, a birthday card, a newspaper clipping of interest, etc.

"Your goal is to make a consistent, personal connection with your prospects. If you can do that and they have the capacity and willingness to give, they will give a gift."

Source: Linda B. Haley, Director of Fund Development Services, Zielinski Companies, St. Louis, MO. Phone (800) 489-2150. E-mail: lhaley@zielinskico.com

2. Help Prospects Visualize Real Ways of Giving

By helping prospects visualize various ways of making major gifts, you allow them to select a comfort level that best meets their individual circumstances. Seeing how others have made gifts moves others closer to giving as well.

And while it is helpful to get the permission of existing donors to allow you to share their giving process with would-be donors, you can also share real-life examples and still retain donors' anonymity.

Here are some examples of ways you can illustrate others' gifts to would-be donors:

1. "We have one couple who established an endowed fund by giving several thousand shares of stock in which they had a very low cost basis. We were able to fund a scholarship in their names and they were able to avoid a huge capital gains tax."

2. "Mary and John Smith wanted to make a sizeable gift but were hesitant as to how to do it. We arrived at a plan together whereby they are contributing $5,000 each year for the next 10 years and have also made our charity the owner and beneficiary of a paid-up $100,000 life insurance policy. They have allowed us to tell others of their gift as a way of encouraging others to do the same."

3. How Passionate Are You?

Believe and you will receive.

Your belief in the value of the organization for which you work is one of the single biggest factors in your fund-raising success. Likewise, the absence of passion will come across to prospective donors and others as an obvious clue that "this charity doesn't deserve my hard-earned money."

Nurture your passion on a daily basis. Meet with and learn from those who benefit from your organization's work. Think about what life would be like for these persons and others in your community if your organization closed its doors. Dream about what you could accomplish with a $10 million gift.

Your ability to inspire yourself — and others — will greatly impact your success in generating major gifts.

4. How Much to Ask For

- To determine how much to ask of an individual who has given consistently over time, multiply his/her average annual gift size times four. Then multiply that amount by five to estimate the total gift that could be made over a five-year period.

5. Prepare Your Solicitation Team

Whenever making a major gift call involving a solicitation team of two or more, be sure each knows his/her role before the meeting takes place. Answer the following questions in advance:

- Who will be making the ask?
- Who is best at answering technical questions regarding the funding project?
- Who will play the primary role in overcoming any donor objections?
- Who should be responsible for any negotiations or instructions regarding topics such as pledge period, gift restrictions, method of payment, etc.?

Although one never knows the twists and turns a conversation might take once the meeting takes place, knowing who's responsible for what in advance helps make for a more smooth and successful solicitation in the end.

6. Upsell Through Comparison

During your last meeting with Jane Doe, she indicated she's thinking of a $50,000 commitment to your campaign, but you know she can do far better than that. How do you move her to that $250,000 gift you had in mind?

One way to do that is by comparing what a $50,000 gift will get her as opposed to one for $250,000. Think of it as comparing a time-share with a private villa in Tuscany.

Share two proposals — one for each gift amount — that compares the benefits of each (naming opportunities, impact on those you serve, impact on your organization's reputation, donor recognition) to show how much more the larger investment will accomplish.

7. Set Aside Time for a Decision

Ever been in the middle of a presentation with a prospect when you notice he/she is continually checking the time?

Take preemptive steps to avoid this uncomfortable scenario from unfolding.

Sylvia Allen, public relations and sales consultant, Allen Consulting (Holmdel, NJ), says to keep the clock-check from happening, take time at the beginning of your call to ask your prospect how much time he/she has set aside for the meeting.

Then — and here's the key — adjust your presentation to take no more than 60 percent of the allotted time.

Why 60 percent?

"Because your prospect's decision to act typically occurs at the end of a meeting, so you want to allow enough time to resolve any remaining issue and reach an agreement," says Allen.

For example, when you first arrive for your meeting ask the prospect, "How much time do you have to spend with me today?" If the prospect responds, "a half-hour or so," that allows 20 minutes for details and background information, and 10 minutes for the close.

"You have to allow yourself time to close but do so from the standpoint of all they're going to give you is the time they said at the beginning of the meeting," says Allen.

This tactic will allow time to close the account by either getting to an immediate "yes," or by possibly overcoming objections and turning a "no" into a "yes."

Results That Matter

Allen says implementation of this technique at your next prospect meeting will result in:

- Better control of your sales time;
- No rushing at the end which can end up in a turn off or worse, a no that cannot be explored; and
- A demonstration of respect for your buyer, resulting in more time for a "yes!"

Source: Sylvia Allen, Public Relations and Sales Consultant, Allen Consulting, Holmdel, NJ. Phone (732) 946-2711. E-mail: Sylvia@allenconsulting.com

8. Be Mindful of the Four Rs

It's helpful to remember that the ideal solicitation experience results in the culmination of the Four Rs:

1. **The right solicitor** — It's important that the match between prospect and solicitor be right.

2. **Asking for the right amount** — Research and previous cultivation should help to answer this question.

3. **For the right purpose** — Again, previous cultivation should point out the funding interests of the prospect.

4. **At the right time** — The prospect may have sold a business and is feeling quite generous or he/she may be going through a divorce in which the thought of a contribution is absent altogether.

9. Major Gift Turnoffs

Don't let your nonprofit become guilty of these major gift turnoffs:

- ✓ Deficit budgets
- ✓ Unprofessional or uninformed staff
- ✓ Unfulfilled promises
- ✓ Negative publicity
- ✓ Lack of a well thought-out strategic plan
- ✓ Poorly maintained facilities
- ✓ A board that lacks leadership and an exemplary level of gift support
- ✓ An invisible CEO
- ✓ Absence of broad-based support

10. Stay Pumped

Your passion — or lack of it — will impact your fundraising success. That's why it's important to keep nurturing a forward-looking outlook.

To help keep yourself optimistic:

- Regularly make calls on both prospects and donors. Nine out of 10 calls will be energizing.

- Mix stewardship calls in with those that may be more challenging. Thanking someone for past support is like a warm-up exercise for solicitation calls that follow.

- Willingly accept donor objections and rejections. Look at them as rebuilding opportunities and steps that bring you closer to your next solicitation success.

11. Phrases That Major Donors Like Hearing

Although there is much more that goes into the making of a major gift than words, there are certain phrases that attract the attention of major gift prospects. Here are a few of them:

"We have experienced more than a decade of balanced budgets."

"We're fortunate to have a reserve in place that, as of yet, we have not had to use."

"We use a conservative percentage of endowment income for annual programs so as to return a portion of it to keep growing our endowment."

"We have a highly reputable group of trustees on our investment committee who include...."

"We never take on a capital project without also raising sufficient endowment to underwrite future operating and maintenance costs of the new or renovated facility."

12. How to Land a Stretch Gift

To receive a stretch gift, a contribution that fulfills a donor's optimum capacity, your organization must ignite the donor's passion for your mission, say Sandra G. Ehrlich, director of fund development services, and Dawn M.S. Miller, senior consultant, Zielinski Companies (St. Louis, MO).

"By listening to and understanding the donor's wants, needs and desires, and sharing who will benefit from this gift and how, your organization will build a case to demonstrate the gift's measurable impact as it ripples into the community," says Ehrlich.

To understand the donor's capacity and willingness to give, you need to know your organization's and prospect's major gift standards.

"Each organization must determine its range, dependent on past donor giving. Whatever the absolute value, it's at that level that the gift begins to stand out from the norm," says Miller.

The primary reason donors give to a nonprofit is belief in its mission, says Ehrlich. "Find out what part of the organization's mission holds the donor's interest and why, and then provide an opportunity for a challenge, stretch gift or one-time gift for a specific purpose that integrates and is consistent with the donor's hopes and dreams for your

organization."

To maximize your ability to receive a stretch gift, answer these questions:

- What in our case holds a special resonance for this donor?
- What values does the donor share?
- How long have they been a donor?
- How did he/she become a donor?
- How is the individual connected to us?
- Who in our agency knows this person?
- Is the donor a volunteer? In what way?
- Is the donor a former or current board member?
- Where do we land in their sphere of philanthropy?

"By reviewing your case for support to determine which projects are most compelling, relevant and urgent for the donor, you'll move the donor closer to your mission and ignite that passion to land the stretch gift," says Ehrlich.

Source: Sandra G. Ehrlich, Director of Fund Development Services, Zielinski Companies, St. Louis, MO. Phone (800) 489-2150. E-mail: sehrlich@zielinskico.com
Dawn M.S. Miller, Senior Consultant, Zielinski Companies, St. Louis, MO. Phone (800) 489-2150.

13. Using 'Back Door' Solicitation May Be Appropriate at Times

One sales technique that has been used during the solicitation process is known as the assumptive close. With this method, the solicitor assumes the prospect will be making a major gift and, instead of making an outright ask, focuses on one or more details associated with the assumed gift.

If, for instance, previous research and visits with a prospect indicate that he/she might be interested in establishing an endowed fund, you may wish to discuss what such a fund would be called (as illustrated below). The act of focusing on what the donor would like to call his/her fund assumes there will be a forthcoming gift.

Illustrations such as the one below are also useful in helping the donor to visualize the eventual reality and impact of making a major gift.

Naming Possibilities
for an Endowed Gift from
John and Elizabeth Widdlesey

The following naming fund possibilities are intended to assist you in selecting a name for your endowment fund. We are not limited to these examples, and you may choose to interchange a part of one example with that of another. The final name you select may also be a reflection of how annual interest from the fund will be used (i.e. scholarship versus recognition fund).

You may also want to consider naming the fund in memory or in honor of a loved one, a respected associate or even an historical figure. The choice is yours.

A. The John and Elizabeth Widdlesey Endowed Fund

B. The John Widdlesey Endowment and The Elizabeth Widdlesey Endowment (two separate funds)

C. The Widdlesey Family Fund

D. The Widdlesey Achievement Fund

E. The Widdlesey Recognition Fund

F. The Widdlesey Scholarship Fund

G. Additional Possibilities _____

_____

_____

---

14. Your Place or Mine?

What percentage of your solicitation calls take place at your own facility versus donors' homes or offices? While it might make sense to solicit donors where they are most comfortable, there are some clear advantages to making the ask on your own turf:

✓ Donors can see your operation at work and become more engaged in seeing and meeting those you serve.

✓ You can better influence the solicitation environment: availability of particular types of audio visual resources, presentation set up, greater accessibility to other offices, staff and more.

✓ You can more adequately illustrate the impact of a major gift and the ways in which the donor will be recognized.

Don't be too quick to eliminate your nonprofit as the best location to make the ask. It's quite possible donors may even prefer that option.

15. Closing Techniques

- **Demonstration Close** — Show a prospective donor what it would be like to make a major gift. For example, if your nonprofit holds an annual reception or luncheon in which all scholarship donors are recognized and meet their scholarship recipients, don't be shy about inviting a handful of others who are considering establishing a named scholarship. Give them a preview of the joy they will experience.

- **Last Chance Close** — Show donors how they will be further ahead by making a pledge now. Example: If it has historically taken a $10,000 pledge to establish a named gift but you plan to make the minimum $25,000, give all prospects the opportunity to establish a named gift before the new policy goes into effect.

17. Judge a Prospect's Propensity to Give

- ■ How do you know when a prospect is moving closer to making a gift? One good measure: He/she begins to ask questions. It's a clear sign that the individual has some level of interest.

16. Planning Is Key To Solicitation Calls

Planning and preparation are key elements to a successful major gift solicitation. As the development officer, it's your job to see that those involved in a solicitation of a major gift are well versed on four key aspects:

1. **The project.** If it's a team solicitation call, at least one member should have a thorough understanding of the funding project and be able to address technical questions that might arise.

2. **The written proposal.** Everyone involved in the solicitation should have an understanding of the proposal's contents: the project description, its budget and the executive summary.

3. **The prospect.** What's the prospect's relationship to your organization? What topics should be avoided? What are his/her primary funding interests?

4. **Each participant's role in the solicitation.** Who will be doing the asking? Who will be prepared to describe the funding opportunity in detail?

18. Learn the Why Behind Each Major Gift

Any time someone makes a major gift, it's important to understand why during that period the decision is made.

Getting a donor to articulate his/her decision to make a major gift at that time has multiple benefits:

1. It helps pinpoint, in the words of the donor, exactly what motivated the gift — a tool that may prove helpful when soliciting future gifts.

2. By enabling major donors to hear themselves verbalizing why they made the gift, the decision to do so becomes even more accepted.

3. Asking donors why they are making such a significant gift is also another way to demonstrate a genuine interest in them. It is an act of stewardship.

Don't hesitate to ask donors repeatedly — in different ways and at different times — why they are making such a generous gift. Most donors will welcome the opportunity to respond again and again.

Ways to Ask 'Why'

Here are some examples of ways to ask a donor why he/she has decided to make a major gift:

"We are so grateful for your generous gift. How did you ultimately arrive at that decision?"

"At what point did you decide this was something you wanted to do?"

"Was there a particular experience in your life that helped you arrive at this decision to make a major gift?"

"I'm always curious when someone makes a gift of this magnitude. What really motivated you to do this?"

"What was it about our institution that drove you to make such a generous commitment?"

19. Four Reasons Why Prospects Say 'No'

Jerry Panas, author, speaker and executive partner with Jerold Panas, Linzy & Partners (Chicago, IL), shares four reasons why a major gift prospect might say no to a solicitation:

1. **It was a mismatch of interests.** The donor isn't interested in the project you are asking them to fund.

2. **The solicitor asked for too much.** If you ask for $100,000 and they're thinking $10,000, it's easier for them to say no than to be embarrassed about saying they will give $10,000.

3. **The solicitor asked for too little.** If it's too small of an amount, the donor may feel you are wasting his or her time.

4. **The solicitor failed to ask for a specific amount.**

Source: Jerry Panas, Author, Lecturer, Executive Partner, Jerold Panas, Linzy & Partners, Chicago, IL. Phone (312) 222-1212

21. Payout Period is Negotiable

As you solicit a prospect for a major gift, don't jump to the payout period for a pledge too quickly. Here's an example of how one might address the issue:

Solicitor: "Mrs. Smith, we would like to invite you to fund this entire project with a gift of $1 million."

Mrs. Smith: "My, but that's a lot of money."

Solicitor: "Mrs. Smith, while we would love it if you could write a check for $1 million, we don't expect you to do that today. We could make arrangements to have the gift paid over a period of years."

22. Do You Suffer From Call Reluctance?

If you suffer from call reluctance, know you're not alone. Even the most seasoned professionals are sometimes hesitant to set appointments and make face-to-face calls.

Understanding call reluctance is a first step in overcoming or diminishing it.

Whether it comes from fear of rejection, a perception that calls are pushy or socially demeaning, or other reasons, all forms of call reluctance can be overcome.

To help diminish your hesitancy to make calls, recognize you can only close gifts by asking for them. The more calls you make, the more successes you will realize. You may never rid yourself of call reluctance, but calls will certainly become easier and more fulfilling with practice. In fact, the majority of calls will energize you.

20. Be Sure Prospects' and Solicitors' Personalities Fit

What systems do you have in place to be sure the right development officer is calling on the right prospect? What if the prospect really doesn't like the representative who has been calling on him/her, but the development officer doesn't want to say anything to his supervisor about poor chemistry because of wanting to get credit for an eventual gift? That happens frequently.

To be sure you have assigned the right development officer to each prospect:

1. Insist on thorough call reports, then make a point to review them carefully.

2. Touch base with each prospect periodically to see if any red flags come up.

3. Consider sending a once-a-year survey to all prospects asking for their input on a number of issues, including their perceptions of staff.

4. Accompany development officers on calls occasionally to see them in action.

By following these steps you will be able to determine if any changes need to be made in who calls on whom.

23. Understand Role of Presentation Tools In Solicitation Calls

What resources do you rely on to help tell your message in face-to-face solicitations?

Thomas Lockerby, vice president for development, Boston College (Chestnut Hill, MA), says the presentation tools they use most often are printed materials.

"We use shorter impact pieces — cultivation pieces about how a gift might make a difference, or stewardship pieces, such as a set of faculty writings or a report from students about the importance of a scholarship," Lockerby says.

They gauge the best timing for introducing these materials on a case-by-case basis with each donor. "I generally introduce written materials during an oral discussion, perhaps in the middle of a conversation with a donor," he says, "although it ultimately depends on the prospect's interests and the nature of the material."

As a general rule, Lockerby says, they don't use electronic tools in major donor presentations: "In very rare cases we might share a PowerPoint presentation if making a strategic impact statement... or an architectural drawing if it is a building discussion."

Source: Thomas B. Lockerby, Vice President for Development, Boston College, Chestnut Hill, MA.

24. Arm Volunteer Callers With Sufficient Calling Information

There's nothing more embarrassing than sending a board member or other volunteer out to make a prospect call, then learning they made a serious blunder because they didn't have ample or correct background information on the person with whom they were meeting. It can be a real nightmare.

To better prepare volunteers for important calls, furnish them with a prospect appointment sheet (see example,

below) that provides all the necessary information they will need to know prior to a visit — contact information (location, phone, etc.), important background information (gift history/purpose) and so forth.

The prospect appointment sheet will improve volunteers' odds for success and make both them and you come across with a higher degree of professionalism.

PROSPECT APPOINTMENT SHEET

Prospective Donor(s) _____ Solicitor(s) _____
_____ _____

Appointment Date _____ Appointment Time _____
Appointment Location _____
Additional Appointment Information _____
_____

Useful Information

Prospect's Occupation _____ Title _____
Place of Work _____ Business Phone _____
E-mail _____ Business Website _____
Residence _____ Home Phone _____
Spouse's Occupation _____ Title _____

Gift History (Optional)   Amount   Gift Designation
2008/09 $ _____   _____
2007/08 $ _____   _____

Suggested Ask Amount (or Range) $ _____

Proposed Gift Designation _____

Additional Comments:

Additional Questions? Contact _____

---

25. Hone Your Presentation Skills

In preparing for a cultivation or solicitation call on a potential donor, pose the so-what question to yourself as a way to focus on key messages you want to convey during that meeting.

Here's an example: "Our agency serves more than 200 children daily."

Playing the prospect role, ask yourself, "So what?" Doing that will help you arrive at a much more convincing, action-oriented message: "It's only because of caring contributors that we are able to assist 200 underprivileged children on a daily basis."

26. Negotiating Strategies

If you have asked a donor for a significant gift and she/he remains hesitant, be prepared to invite a combination outright and planned gift:

"Mrs. Prospect, let me suggest another approach you may wish to consider. If you were to make a five-year pledge of $X and also make provisions to add to the fund after your lifetime, we could attain that goal we've discussed."

27. Don't Be Intimidated by Presentations to Gift Committees

Meeting with one prospect at a time can be challenging enough, but making a presentation before a business gift committee can be downright intimidating. Instead of having to sell one person, you have to sell the majority of those present. Each representative has different interests, varying likes and dislikes.

To put your best foot forward for a group presentation:

1. **Learn as much as you can about those who make up the group** prior to your meeting. What are their positions in the company? Who among your organization's board and close friends might know any of these persons and be able to give you more insight into them?

2. **Understand past funding projects.** If you can learn anything about the group's past giving decisions, that may give you some insight to the approach you should take. Also, determine if any funding guidelines are available.

3. Although you should be communicating and making visual contact with each committee member during your presentation, **prepare a compelling message just as you would if you were approaching one individual.** If your rationale for support is solid, it will withstand the test of multiple individuals' judgments. Also, your message should not come across as canned.

4. **Treat each member of the gifts team with equal respect and attention.** Speak to every member of the group and answer each person's questions with the same attention to detail. Provide sufficient handouts for everyone present and be sure that each attendee can easily see the visuals included in your presentation.

5. **Be genuine.** Be a good listener and, most importantly, be yourself.

28. Responding to Prospect's Comment: 'That's a Lot of Money!'

You've been cultivating a major gift prospect for nearly 18 months. You know of one instance in which she has made a $100,000 gift to another charity, but you also believe she's capable of giving much more than that. Together, you have determined her funding interests, but no dollar figure has been discussed. Today's the big day: You present her with a proposal for a $350,000 gift. She glances at it, notices the dollar amount and, in amazement, says: "That's a lot of money!"

How do you respond at that moment? What can you possibly say? Here are some options:

1. **Wait for the prospect's next comment before saying anything.** Silence can be deadly, but it can also be wise

to wait for a follow-up comment. Although the prospect could say "that's too much for me to give," she may also make a more hopeful response: "It is a lot of money, but I guess it's not out of the realm of possibility."

2. **Be prepared to negotiate.** Respond with a comment such as: "Yes, that is a very generous investment, but please keep in mind that it could be given over a period of time."

3. **Emphasize the gift's impact and its benefits.** "Not only will the annual interest from this endowed fund benefit some 20 children each year, the named fund will be a lasting tribute in honor of your parents for generations to come."

29. Take Body Language Into Consideration

Successful development professionals include those who can key into prospect behavior and body language. They know what to say, how to say it and when to say it, based on their listening skills and ability to discern a person's behavior.

Part of understanding human behavior includes sensitivity to body language. In fact, as much as 65 percent of communication can be nonverbal.

When you pose a question, how does a person's body language tell you what he/she is really thinking?

Here are some tips to help you interpret another's body language:

• **Reflecting on something you said:** head tilted slightly

with eyes looking up; hand to cheek or finger stroking chin.

• **Defensiveness, disapproval:** minimal facial expressions or eye contact; frown; arms crossed.

• **Receptive:** head nodding; occasional smile; consistent eye contact; animated.

• **Boredom, indifference:** lack of eye contact; shifting positions frequently; checking the time.

Keep in mind that while reading other person's body language is important, being aware of what your body language is saying to others is just as important.

30. Help Your Team Anticipate Questions

When enlisting the help of others in making a team solicitation, hold a pre-call briefing session that includes a review of possible questions or issues that might be raised by the donor. Equally important, know who will respond to them.

Depending on the project, examples of questions might include:

- How do I know my endowment fund would consistently return five percent on an annual basis?

- What if your organization gets into trouble financially or ceases to exist? What would happen to my gift then?

- How much is your board giving to this campaign?

- How did you come up with that gift amount for me?

32. Who Should Make Up Your Solicitation Team?

The "1-2-3 closing rule" for major gift solicitation is one that will help guide you and your team through the asking process. The solicitation team — whether or not all members are present during the ask — should consist of:

1. **The primary solicitor** — The individual who will be making the ask.

2. **The manager** — The staff person charged with overseeing research, cultivation and solicitation of major gift prospects.

3. **Any key secondary player(s)** — Someone close to the prospect who may accompany the solicitor or provide valuable background information, or perhaps someone who is key to the funding project and knows answers to technical questions regarding the use of the gift.

34. Fundraising Truisms

✓ Money is the root of all excellence.

✓ You can only get money from people who have money.

✓ Donors don't make major gifts because of your nonprofit's needs. They make such gifts based on their own needs.

✓ Recognize that logic facilitates a major gift, but emotion motivates it.

31. Ask With Confidence

Repeat this out loud: "I would like to invite you to make a $3 million investment in [name of your organization]." Was it easy? Did you feel any trepidation as "$3 million" rolled off your tongue?

Know this: Would-be donors pick up on your body language, your tone of voice and other clues that convey your beliefs and level of confidence.

If you say "$3 million" like you believe it's more than you should be asking for, the individual will catch that and probably respond in a corresponding way: "You're asking for way too much!" If, on the other hand, you extend an invitation for a $3 million gift with confidence, the prospect will know that you expect he/she is fully capable of making a gift at that level.

33. Proposals Legitimize Your Request

While there may be times when a written proposal is unnecessary, a formal written proposal — even if only one page in length — adds a certain leveraging quality to the solicitation process.

Written proposals should:

- Describe in detail how the gift will be used

- Delineate donor benefits

- Suggest naming opportunities

- Clarify perceptions between prospects and solicitors

- Serve as continual reminders in the absence of staff visits

The timing for delivery of a written proposal may vary: It can be presented in person or it can be developed and sent following a visit. The timing and method of delivery depend on the circumstances surrounding it.

35. How to Respond to Decision Delays

Got a prospect who's putting off responding to your major gift request? While it's best not to rush the process, you can take these steps to move toward a positive outcome:

1. **Allow some breathing time.** Suggest a time at which you will get back to the prospect after he/she has had an opportunity to more fully weigh the options, for example: "I will plan to call and set up an appointment in a week." Then follow up your visit with a letter confirming the upcoming visit and pointing out the value and benefits of a positive decision.

2. **Pull in your big guns.** Bring along your CEO or an influential board member or another major donor who will add a higher level of urgency to a positive outcome.

36. Keep a List of Techniques to Remember

When you make calls on major gift prospects, you no doubt complete a call report following each visit. But have you ever begun a separate list of cultivation or sales techniques that work well for you? Perhaps you shared the names of other individuals who established a named endowed fund at your charity and, in doing so, saw the prospect's interest begin to pick up. Or maybe you were part of a calling team and something your partner said helped to close the gift.

Aside from your call report, begin a list of tried-and-tested presentation or solicitation methods that have worked for you. Include the date, the prospect on whom you

called, the technique used and how that technique proved invaluable. It's amazing how soon we sometimes forget to rely on tools that have worked well in the past. With a techniques-to-remember list, you can periodically refer to it — perhaps prior to each call — to refresh your memory of the sales choices you have at hand.

Some techniques might be universally beneficial to anyone who uses them. Others may be more suited to your particular style. In any event, you will find the list to be a helpful way to hone your sales skills over time. For examples, see below.

SALES AND CULTIVATION TECHNIQUES WORTH REMEMBERING

Name _____

DATE	PROSPECT	USEFUL TECHNIQUE	WHY IT WORKED
2/5/08	M & S Wiedern	Shared a scale of gifts chart	Hesitant about suggesting a specific amount
5/3/08	J Galbraith	Cited Molone Scholarship donors	Prospect was thinking outright gift only; now considering outright and planned gift.

37. Think You're Not Getting Through? Don't Give Up

One hospital's major gifts officer couldn't help but notice one of her community's philanthropists had made seven-figure gifts to some highly reputable charities outside of the community. The gift officer wondered: "How can I convince her that our hospital is worthy of such support?"

Since the philanthropist was somewhat of a loner, the development officer could find no one who could help make an introduction. The development officer sent a letter of introduction and a few days later attempted to phone the woman to set an appointment, but she would never pick up the phone. After several attempts, the development officer began sending letters with handwritten notes as a continuing effort to meet with the woman. No response. Still, she kept sending notes, spoon-feeding the woman with information that would help her understand the hospital's critical role in the community.

One day when the development officer stopped by a local clothing store after work, she spotted the woman in the store. As much as she hesitated to approach the prospect in such an unlikely place, she decided to step up and make an introduction: "Mrs. Ford, my name is Lori Lane. I'm with the Hantla Medical Center."

"Oh yes," replied the woman. "I've enjoyed learning

about your hospital's work. I've spoken to my trust officer and you should be hearing from him soon."

The development officer was amazed to learn that her messages had, in fact, been heard. Two weeks later the hospital received a check for $1 million.

There are times when you will feel like giving up on a prospect. But don't. You never know when your persistence will pay off in a big way.

38. Listening Skills Tips

To become a better listener when meeting with would-be donors:

1. Lean forward to pretend you're listening and you really will listen more closely.

2. Repeat back something the prospect said. Knowing you want to repeat something forces you to listen more thoughtfully. By repeating what was just said, the prospect may reveal additional clues that will help when it's time to make the ask.

39. Avoid These Team Solicitation Pitfalls

If you're making calls in teams of two or three — one staff person and one or two volunteers — be sure the secondary solicitors are fully prepared. As helpful as it can be to have a team rather than one person make the call, an unprepared team member can unintentionally dismantle what's been accomplished.

Avoid having a team member who:

- Fails to listen fully to the prospect.

- Has little or no background information about the prospect.

- Has yet to make a generous commitment to your organization.

- Talks too much.

- Lacks understanding about the project you wish to have funded.

- Isn't familiar with key facts and history regarding your organization and its work.

- Has little or no previous involvement with your organization.

40. Methods for Determining Ask Amount

Various rules of thumb serve as guides in setting an appropriate ask amount. Keep in mind, however, these are intended as guides only. Having said that, here is one method for determining the ask amount based on a five-year pledge period:

Take the individual's average yearly contribution and multiply that by 20. If, for instance, someone was contributing $1,000 on an annual basis, you would take that number times 20 to get the ask amount of $20,000. Because this is for a capital campaign that seeks a higher level of sacrificial giving, the request is based on an ask that is four times the donor's annual gift to be given annually for five years (4 x $1,000 x 5 years gives you $20,000).

You may choose to increase or decrease that sacrificial multiplier — in this example, 4 — depending on the prospect's financial capability and proclivity to give.

41. Positive Thinking — What You Think Is What You'll Get

If your regular work day is consumed by feelings of stress, defeat, resentment and powerlessness, the likelihood of your being able to raise major gifts will be negligible. If, on the other hand, you begin each day with determination and exuberance, you will surprise yourself at what can be accomplished.

Eighty percent of fundraising success is the result of passionate, positive thinking; 10 percent is the result of practicing the science and art of fundraising; and 10 percent is based on luck.

Consciously take steps to become a more positive thinker in your everyday life. Know that you can make believers out of would-be donors. Be passionate about your cause. Face your fears head on. Realize that each failure along the way is one step closer to your next major victory.

You are the key to fundraising success — not the economy, not competition from other nonprofits. You. You are the key to achieve success.

If you strive to operate from a positive, can-do frame of mind in spite of would-be obstacles, there's no question about it — you will succeed beyond belief. It's only a matter of time.

42. Go Back to Those Who Rejected Your Initial Request

When you're in the midst of a capital campaign and someone declines your invitation to make a gift, don't write that person off entirely. Instead, develop a personalized response letter that thanks the individual for considering a gift and leaves the door open for a later approach. After all, the timing of your request may have been an issue.

Keep sending campaign updates to those nonparticipants as the campaign progresses. Then, as you move into the last quarter of your campaign, probably months after you made the initial request, approach those prospects once again for a face-to-face update and one last opportunity to be a part of "this great effort." You may be surprised at the number of people who will hop on the bandwagon to support your cause and campaign.

Dear Susan and Tom:

Even though you chose not to participate in our capital campaign at this time, I want you to know how much we appreciate your having given the matter consideration.

We really value you as members of our "family" and will continue to keep you updated on the campaign's progress and other news of interest.

43. Emphasize Opportunity You're Offering Prospects

When asking for a major gift, underscore the fact that you're giving the prospect a unique opportunity to make a positive difference by using wording such as:

"Mrs. Clark, a scholarship in your husband's memory will benefit our students not only today, but for generations to come. The name 'Mr. Jon Clark' will stand for a belief in our school's ability to make a positive impact on our community's future."

"Robert, your matching gift will do two amazing things: First, it will motivate folks who are on the fence to write a check, since their gift will now be doubled. And second, the announcement of your challenge gift will send the powerful message that this campaign is worthy of the support of a man of your stature."

"Mr. and Mrs. Ortega, I'm calling because I wanted to be sure you were among the first to hear about this. As you may know, we're just in the beginning design phases of our new art center. I'd love to sit down with you and our architect to give you a feel for how amazing it will be when it's done! We can also visit about how to get you in early on the option of having an art classroom or display gallery named in your honor."

45. Closing Techniques

- **Testimonial Close** — Bring along a donor who has made a gift of the same type and size that you hope to secure from the prospect at hand. Ask the donor to share his/her thoughts and benefits from having made a significant gift.

- **Sudden-death Close** — After repeated visits to a prospect who can never make up his/her mind about any number of gift alternatives (e.g., gift size, use of gift, pledge period), bring a one-page proposal that spells out all of those specifics. Include a line at the bottom for the prospect's signature. Using this technique to bring those decisions to a head in print should help move the prospect off dead center and closer to making a gift.

- **The Triple Option Close** — This technique involves giving the prospect three gift choices: one that's two to three times as much as you hope to receive, one that's somewhat higher than you expect and a final option that's your target amount.

- **The Comparative Close** — Be ready to share anecdotes of donors who have made similar gifts for similar purposes. Sharing real examples of major gifts helps the prospect overcome reluctance to make a major gift investment.

44. Launch Trial Balloons To Test Prospects' Readiness

As you proceed through the cultivation stages and near a formal solicitation, don't hesitate to test the water to get some sense of a prospect's readiness to make a gift. Carefully worded questions should provide answers that will help you determine if the timing is right to extend an invitation.

Here are examples of trial balloon questions:

✓ If you were to make a significant gift at some point, what aspects of our agency would you most prefer to support?

✓ Of the funding projects we reviewed during our last get-together, what intrigued you most?

✓ Have you ever considered establishing a naming gift of some sort?

✓ At this point, where do you see yourself on this scale of giving chart?

46. Time Your Asks

When trying to determine whether an individual is ready to be asked for a major gift, says Lisa M. Dietlin, president and CEO of Lisa M. Dietlin & Associates (Chicago, IL), look for whether he/she is:

- **Invested in all ways in the organization.** The individual should have shown his/her interests by participating in events, writing checks, serving on boards and by expressing an interest in the organization's programs and projects.

- **Going above and beyond to help the organization.** Are they not only volunteering for an event, but also inviting other people to attend?

- **Increasing their donations without being asked.**

- **Asking you outright what they can do to help.** If this happens, be prepared with an answer: "I want to talk to you about a gift that would significantly impact this organization…"

- **Saying both directly and indirectly that they are ready and able to help.** Listen for statements about a prospect's life events and understand what they mean for the prospect and your organization. For example, if the prospect tells you they have sold their business, they are telling you what they are capable of doing for your organization.

Source: Lisa M. Dietlin, President and CEO, Lisa M. Dietlin & Associates, Chicago, IL. Phone (773) 772-4465. E-mail: tara@lmdietlin.com

47. Team Solicitation Worksheet Helps Gear Up for Call

The team approach is often a good choice for major gift solicitation.

Often, a two-person team will include a paid development officer along with a board member, volunteer or employee of the organization who can field more technical questions about the funding project. And, of course, both team members can be paid staff, volunteers or board members.

Whatever combination you choose for a team solicitation, it's important for each team member to know his/her role. Discussing who will say what in advance makes for a more seamless presentation and reduces the likelihood of mistakes.

And since one person is generally responsible for leading the conversation and making the ask while the other serves to support the primary solicitor, it's wise to review who will say what before your meeting. Also, brainstorm to anticipate and craft answers to any questions or obstacles that may arise.

A team solicitation worksheet (like the one shown here), that both team members fill out ahead of time can help them better prepare for a successful solicitation.

Team Solicitation Worksheet

Prospect _____

Team Solicitors:
   Primary Solicitor _____

   Support _____

Solicitation Date _____ Time _____ Location _____

Ask Amount or Range: $ _____

Call Plan

	Lead	Support
Introductory remarks		
Rapport building		
Topic Lead-in		
Purpose of solicitation		
Project description/background		
Questions/answers		
Solicitation		
Prospect response		
Solicitor response (Objections/negotiations)		
Pledge commitment/next steps		
Request for referrals (optional)		
Thank you		

48. Solicitation Calls: What Follows After Hearing Yes?

Your donor says yes to a major gift? Great! But be sure to take the proper steps to confirm the pledge before leaving the donor's office.

Jeff Miller, president and CEO, Junior Achievement of Central Indiana, Inc. (Indianapolis, IN), keeps a pledge form with him and uses it to capture the details of the gift before he leaves. He also makes sure the donor signs the form before he leaves.

The pledge form (shown in abbreviated format, below) includes what kind of recognition the donor will receive and a basic schedule of payments and dates.

"I'm quite detailed at this time because it is a lot tougher to go back if things are not very clear," says Miller. "I've learned that the word 'raised' on a matching pledge can mean something very different to the donor than it does to the recipient. To me, 'raised' means a signed pledge agreement. In Indiana, a signed pledge agreement is a legally enforceable instrument. However, a misunderstanding of one word can make a huge difference."

Once he returns to the office and types up the form, Miller makes a point to send, or if possible, hand-deliver, a copy as another opportunity to get face to face with the donor to further build the relationship.

Diana Humphrey, senior director of development, major gifts, Indiana University Kelley School of Business (Bloomington, IN), says that as soon as a donor says "yes," she gets the gift agreement or pledge form signed by the donor, school and foundation officials.

"I also talk to the donor about what their expectations are and what we have to offer them with regard to stewardship of their gift," she says. "For example, if it is a scholarship gift, we will describe the stewardship process for that gift, e.g., a thank-you from the student receiving the scholarship, an invitation to the annual scholarship lunch, etc."

The pledge form also includes information about matching funds; when the donor would like courtesy reminders and whether officials may announce the gift.

Upon receipt of a major gift, Humphrey says, "We will immediately send thank-you letters to the donor. Depending on the size of the gift, the dean will also send a letter."

The school, depending on the size of the gift and if the donor is agreeable, will also issue a press release about the gift and write an article for the school's website, she says.

Source: Jeff Miller, President & CEO, Junior Achievement of Central Indiana, Inc., Indianapolis, IN. Phone (317) 252-5900, ext. 202. E-mail: jeff@jaindy.org
Diana Humphrey, Senior Director of Major Gifts, Indiana University, Bloomington, Kelley School of Business, Bloomington, IN. Phone (812) 855-6997. E-mail: humphre@indiana.edu

The president and CEO of Junior Achievement of Central Indiana, Inc. (Indianapolis, IN) keeps this form on hand to officially capture specifics when a prospect says yes to a major gift:

Content not available in this edition

49. Your Proposals Should Quantify Gifts' Impact

When submitting proposals to individuals and businesses, be sure some section of the document quantifies the impact a donor's gift will have on your organization and those served by it. It's not enough to be subjective if you really want to positively influence a prospect's decision-making process. Foundations often demand proposals that quantify a grant's outcomes; why shouldn't individuals and businesses deserve that same level of accountability?

Your proposal should attempt to quantify a gift's impact, whether it is intended for capital improvements, endowment, programs, personnel, equipment or other uses.

To assist you in drafting a proposal that quantifies outcomes, put yourself in the place of the donor. If you were to contribute a $1 million naming gift for a new auditorium, for instance, what would you like to know that it will accomplish? Rather than vague wording that says "this wonderful asset will be used throughout the year," focus the proposal on measurable outcomes.

THE AGNES K. KNOWLES AUDITORIUM

Anticipated Impact

✓ The auditorium will comfortably seat 500 people.

✓ The facility will host approximately 60 cultural and educational events throughout the year based on planning to date:
- Music events......................20   (Open to the public)
- Lectures............................15   (Open to the public)
- Seminars...........................10
- Drama productions.........4   (Open to the public)
- Student assemblies..........5

✓ Anticipated average audience reach: 75 miles

---

50. Help Prospects Visualize Their Gifts' Impact

Selling something that won't exist until it's paid for can be challenging — a new building or a new program, for instance. How can you convince someone to put up $100,000 or more for something that he/she can't see, touch or fully experience?

Here's one way to do so: Use the past to sell the future. Help your prospects distinguish between now and then, before and after.

Whether you're selling a new building or a new program, point out what is being accomplished and not accomplished in the absence of the funding project. Then articulate — in terms they can understand — the impact the project will have once it is up and running. How will the completion of the project impact peoples' lives? How will it further your organization's reputation and enhance the community or region? What will the facility or program provide that currently is missing?

Selling dreams requires appealing to both the mind and the heart with heavier emphasis on the heart. Architectural drawings, facts, figures and charts help satisfy the intellectual needs of the prospect. Stories of how lives will be positively impacted, the good a new building or program will accomplish, appeal to the prospect's emotions.

Finally, sell smaller dreams first. If you're building a new science center, for instance, point out the real life benefits of a particular lab rather than dwelling on the benefits of the entire facility. Spoon-feeding smaller components of the overall project helps the prospect to better visualize and understand its multiple benefits.

51. Offer Gift Ranges?

Some fundraising consultants say you should avoid offering a prospect a gift range (e.g., $50,000 to $100,000), since the prospect will generally choose the bottom end of the suggested range.

52. Regularly Share Naming Opportunities

Who says you have to be in the midst of a capital campaign to offer naming opportunities for existing facilities (and rooms and offices within those facilities)?

Make a list of all buildings and spaces within buildings that have not been named, assigning a required gift value to each. Then selectively share the list with prospects who may wish to endow and name certain spaces.

53. Solicitation Tips

- When setting an appointment to call on a prospect for support, **be up front about who will be present.** If, for instance, you will be accompanied by one or two others, share their names with the prospect in advance.

- **Employ the changing-the-scale technique.** Before you arrive at the ask amount, dangle a much larger "price tag" in front of the prospect. Then quickly summarize the benefits of the gift and conclude with a more modest ask amount. Your request will be palatable, and you will be asking for your original target figure.

- **Give would-be donors a choice.** Rather than asking for one amount, offer the prospect a choice of three figures: one significantly more than you would expect, one moderately more and one that is what you expect. Then ask the prospect which of the three works best. This subtle approach avoids a yes-or-no response.

- **When soliciting a married couple, pay equal attention to both spouses.** The most vocal of the two will most likely not make the final decision alone, and each will be influenced by the other. Be alert to the body language of the quieter of the two, and head off any reservations by encouraging the less-verbal one to voice questions or opinions, being sure to thoroughly address those issues before a final decision is made.

- **Practice closing incrementally.** Convince your prospects to make smaller decisions leading up to the ask. **Example:** If the goal is to establish a $50,000 scholarship, convince the prospect to consider what it might be named, how often scholarships would be awarded, who would qualify, etc.

54. Key Elements of a Proposal

The purpose of the major gift funding proposal is to present the case for support and the campaign's supporting materials to the prospect, says Jodie Nolan, vice president of gift planning services, Paul J. Strawhecker, Inc. (Omaha, NE).

"The funding proposal describes everything about the organization and the funding request: the mission, the project, and what their gift will fund," Nolan says. "It allows you to have something tangible to hand to the prospect. It also helps them in making their decision because it serves as an outline and how the gift will help the organization."

Nolan shares the main elements of a major gift funding proposal:

- Cover letter to the individual prospect
- Summary document with the case for support
- Architectural drawings (if applicable)
- Project budget
- Who the other donors are
- List of board members and/or volunteers
- Audit, financial statement (depending on the gift size)
- Letter of intent

"You should include a letter of intent, but do not leave it with the prospect if they have not committed," she says. "This will give you an opportunity to return for further discussion concerning a decision."

Source: Jodie Nolan, Vice President of Gift Planning Services, Paul J. Strawhecker, Inc., Omaha, NE.
Phone (402) 556-5785. E-mail: jodie@pjstraw.com

55. Donor Resistance Could Be Result of Poor Cultivation

You did your research, visited the donor many times, asked a lot of questions, and, listening to the answers, came up with a very specific ask, including a gift size, purpose and time line. Yet, when you said, "Will you make X gift to X program over X amount of time?" the donor showed some reluctance to say yes.

What should you do?

Kent Stroman, president, Stroman & Associates (Bartlesville, OK), a consulting firm specializing in major fundraising campaigns, suggests you ask the donor what about the request he or she is not ready to say yes to — and then listen.

Listen for signs that may indicate the donor is having a change of heart, you are asking for the wrong amount or at the wrong time.

"Use strategic questions to help the donor get comfortable with the ask," Stroman says. "For example, ask the donor: 'When would be a good time to make this decision?' If you still see some resistance/reluctance on the part of the donor, ask him/her 'What would have to happen in order to say yes to a major gift or opportunity like this?'"

Before making the ask, says Stroman, you should have asked the donor a number of exploring questions and done a lot of listening, looking for and working out any areas of resistance.

"Lots of conversations need to happen before making the ask," he says. In these visits, "the donor should have informed you how the proposal should be shaped. If, once the ask is made, the donor is still showing some resistance, it could be because you asked the right questions, but didn't listen carefully to the answers. Go back and ask your questions again, listening for answers you didn't hear before."

Source: M. Kent Stroman, President, Stroman & Associates, Bartlesville, OK. Phone (866) 787-6626.
E-mail: StromanConsults@aol.com

56. Financially Secure Nonprofits Deserve Support, Too

If you have the good fortune to represent a financially solid charity, you may come into contact with those who think you don't need their support.

"Why should I support you? You don't need my money!"

When that happens, how do you respond? Do you have a repertoire of comebacks for such negative thinking?

If they are not already among your comebacks, feel free to add any of these:

✓ The generosity of people like you has allowed us to experience decades of balanced budgets.

✓ Think of us as an equity investment. When you invest in us, you know your gift will be well-managed.

✓ The fact that we have a track record of sound fiscal management does not lessen or negate the needs of those we serve.

✓ I will gladly share a list of 2,000 donors who believe we are worthy and deserving of their support, and we would be honored to count you among them.

58. Practice Makes Perfect: Don't Shy Away From Asking

When it comes to soliciting major gifts, remember this: It's better to ask and make mistakes than it is to wait forever in your quest to perfect the close.

Will you make mistakes? Of course. Even the most accomplished solicitors make mistakes. That's how we learn. But don't let those mistakes stop you from pursuing major gifts. Keep asking and learning from your previous asks.

In addition to writing up a trip or call report after each solicitation, take the time to make some personal notes. List what went right during the call. Then write down what went wrong. Be honest with yourself.

By evaluating each call, you will learn that it's not so much your style or even your knowledge that determines a potential gift. Rather, it's your determination to keep asking.

60. Speak With Confidence

When talking to donors and probable donors, avoid using words and phrases that convey uncertainty. Instead of saying "I'll try..." say "I will." Investors want to know they are dealing with a confident individual.

57. How to Lead Up to the Close

What do you talk about just before popping the question? What can you say that will set the stage for that final ask?

Although your answers will vary somewhat depending on individual circumstances, it is safe to say that, if you've done all of your cultivation homework in prior meetings, your comments leading up to the ask should involve reiterating some key elements of what's been said before.

Some examples of what you might have said in leading up to the close include:

• I know that based on our previous discussions, you have indicated an interest in participating in this campaign at some level.

• In past visits you have expressed a particular interest in funding [name of project]....

• Before I invite you to make your commitment, let me say that, in my opinion, your gift will clearly set the pace for those that follow.

• [Name of charity] has set out to achieve some extraordinary accomplishments over the next several years. And if we are to do that, it will require extraordinary sacrifice of everyone associated with our institution.

59. Offer Language That Calls for Major Gifts

As you prepare to solicit persons capable of making six- and seven-figure gifts, it's worth contemplating the choice of messages and phrases you plan to convey during those all-important meetings.

Some examples of appropriate language may include:

• There is frankly no one more capable than you who can make this vision a reality.

• The ultimate success of this campaign will require an unprecedented gift.

• Your level of investment will set the pace for those gifts that follow.

• You are among that select handful of individuals who possess the ability to....

• Never in the history of our institution have we attempted to achieve such an extraordinary goal.

61. Know These Four Solicitation Myths

While there are obvious principles you can follow in soliciting major gifts, it's important to recognize that there are always exceptions to the rule. Here are four so-called principles that often have such exceptions:

Myth 1: Always ask for a specific gift amount. There may be times when you're pushing your luck to ask for a specific amount. Instead, refer to a chart of gift ranges and ask "Where do you see yourself on this scale of giving?"

Myth 2: Never re-approach a prospect who refused to make a pledge or gift. Recognize that "no" sometimes means "not now." Circumstances may have changed since your last request for support.

Myth 3: Always include both spouses when soliciting a gift. It's important to be sensitive to the primary spouse's signals. Perhaps he/she is the key decision maker and insisting that both spouses be involved would be a mistake.

Myth 4: Never solicit a prospect without having involved and engaged him/her in your organization and its work. Some people may believe in your cause sufficiently to give but don't have the time or inkling for further involvement.

63. Deal With And Learn From Rejection

Even though you may never fully accept rejection, it's important to learn from it.

After all, rejection happens to even the very best solicitors. If you're not experiencing rejection, you're not making a sufficient number of calls.

Whenever you experience rejection, learn from it in these and other ways:

1. **After leaving a prospect who turned you down, briefly analyze the call.** What might you do differently another time? Was timing an issue? Could it be that this prospect is not inclined to be philanthropic toward any deserving cause?

2. **Include rejection conclusions in your call report.** Those historical notes will be of value for future calls, and the act of recording those observations helps draw closure to any negative thinking on your part.

3. **Don't take rejection personally.** You can expect a certain number of refusals just as you can expect a certain number of successes. Keep in mind that each rejection puts you that much closer to your next successful solicitation.

62. Learn to Spot Timing Issues

Sometimes a donor's objection is more a function of timing as illustrated in the following example:

Solicitor: "Janice, I want to invite you to support our capital campaign with a $25,000 gift."

Donor: "As much as I would love to do that, my youngest still has two more years of college, so it's more than I can handle right now."

Solicitor: "I can certainly appreciate that. To help you through that, we can set up your pledge with smaller payments for the next two years and then increase them following that period."

It would be easy to cave in and assume a gift isn't possible based on timing, but by structuring the pledge to accommodate the donor's circumstances, the needs of both parties can be met.

64. Development Officer As Solicitor

It makes good sense for the development officer to serve as a team member during a solicitation call, even if he/she does not serve as the solicitor.

Under ideal circumstances, the development officer:

✓ Has a long-term association with the prospect
✓ Possesses good listening skills
✓ Has experience in directing the conversation
✓ Knows how to ask for the gift
✓ Recognizes steps that should occur following the request

65. Clarify Who You Want to Solicit

One business contact — the CEO of a company, for example — can often be the same decision maker for various sources of gifts, such as personal, corporate, foundation, etc. If you're hoping to receive multiple gifts through the same contact, clarify your position up front rather than making multiple requests over time. Otherwise, it gives the appearance of going to the well too often.

Here's one way of articulating your desire for multiple gifts through the same source:

"Mr. Davis, I'm here to talk to you about seeking support from three sources: a personal gift, a corporate gift and a gift from your foundation."

66. Include an Executive Summary With All Proposals

Do you follow a standard outline when crafting major gift proposals? Whether you do or not, make a point to include an executive summary at the beginning of your written document. The reason for that is two-fold:

1. If written properly, a proposal summary will tempt the potential donor to read on. As you draft the summary, attempt to view it through the eyes of the would-be donor. In 200 words or less, what can you say that will captivate the reader? Obviously, the proposed name of the fund or building project will draw attention. The way you describe the impact of the donor's gift may also come into play. If the donor has an obvious interest in the future growth of a proposed endowment fund or the annual interest from it, for instance, you may want to devote more wordage to the way the gift will be invested and how it relates to your overall endowment.

2. Summaries will also help to insure readers see the document's big picture if they choose not to read anything more. Knowing that could happen, the summary should include the ask amount, what the realization of that gift would accomplish and the benefits to the donor for making that gift a reality. Do not include the

payout period for your request; that's an item that can be negotiated as the gift is finalized.

Content not available in this edition

67. Prepare Board Members, Volunteers for Team Solicitations

Before asking board members or other volunteers to participate in donor solicitation calls, know the roles everyone will play, says Marion Conway, principal, Marion Conway Consulting (Verona, NJ).

"Does the board member/volunteer represent the link to the potential donor as a friend, business associate or alumni of the same college, or does he or she represent an added representative from the organization?" Conway says. "Their role may be different depending on their relationship with the potential donor."

In either case, board members/volunteers should share with the prospect their connection with the organization and passion for its mission, their personal relationship with its work and events, how it benefits their family and the community.

Discussing major goals of the strategic plan and the vision for the organization's future is also valuable and appropriate, Conway says.

Meet before the solicitation call to discuss these roles so there are no surprises at the call, she says. Cover the type of questions they will answer and which questions you will handle: "For example, if you have developed a list of program options that the donor might support, the board member or volunteer may help figure out which options are most likely to appeal to the donor."

If the board member/volunteer has a personal relationship with the potential donor, it is appropriate for him or her to make the ask, says Conway, because it can be done in an informal and personal way. "If the board member/ volunteer does not have a personal relationship with the donor, it is better for you to make the ask. In either case you should know what the specific ask will be."

Source: Marion Conway, Marion Conway Consulting, Verona, NJ. Phone (973) 239-8937. E-mail: mc@marionconwayconsulting.com

68. Understand Decision Process

The theory has been proven time and again: Most consumer purchases are first motivated by an individual's emotions and then rationalized. Once the information has been weighed, however, the final decision is based on emotion.

Take the purchase of a house as an example. First, the potential buyer looks at a house and asks: "Does it feel right? Could I picture myself living here?" Those emotional reactions are followed by more cognitive thoughts: "Can I afford this? What will my monthly payments be?" But before the final purchase is made, the buyer again thinks emotionally: "What do I like about this house? How will I feel about this home, this location?"

The process is much the same with major gift giving. First the donor thinks about what it would be like to make a sizable gift, followed by more pragmatic thoughts: "Can I afford to do this? What will be the tax consequences of this gift?" But finally the donor again turns to emotional thoughts:

"How would it feel to establish a naming gift or to help those in need or to have my name on that building?"

Although pragmatic thoughts such as tax consequences may come into play, most donors' decisions are driven by their emotions, be they altruistic, ego or some other psychological need.

70. Learn to 'Bridge' Closing Techniques

If you find yourself in the middle of closing a gift and perceive the solicitation is not moving as smoothly as you'd prefer, know how to move on to another closing method.

Going into a solicitation knowing you have a variety of closing techniques available lets you test one method and, if necessary, move to more effective ones. One technique involves asking the prospect a question that, if answered, implies a commitment:

> Solicitor: "Jim, a gift at this level will allow you to establish a named endowment. Will you want your name on the fund or is there some other significant person in your life you would prefer to recognize?"

The response calls for a confirmation to make the gift. If however, the solicitor senses the prospect has not yet decided to make a pledge, it's helpful to know how to "bridge" to additional techniques that may result in the desired commitment:

> Solicitor: "If you are hesitant about how such a fund would be named, let me share examples of what others have done in selecting a name they found to be most appropriate...."

69. Avoid Solicitation Slip-ups

Whether you're a seasoned development professional or new to the job, avoid making these 10 solicitation mistakes:

1. **Not asking.** No ask, no get. It's that simple.

2. **Not being direct.** Don't hint at what you want. Look your prospect in the eyes and make your request clear.

3. **Apologizing or begging.** Always remember: Making a gift is a privilege, not charity.

4. **Being unfamiliar with your nonprofit's finances.** If you're talking money, you should know about your employer's finances.

5. **Aiming too low.** Don't underestimate a donor's giving potential. Ask for more than you expect to receive.

6. **Failing to ask your own family, friends and colleagues.** If you believe in your cause, why wouldn't you approach your closest allies?

7. **Not being up front.** Be open and honest about asking for funds.

8. **Asking only once.** Know that if a prospect says no, it might mean not now. Be persistent.

9. **Not asking for what you want.** If a project requires $5,000 to complete, don't ask for less. Go for it.

10. **Stopping with the first yes.** If a donor has contributed once, don't assume that's it for the year. That should be their decision, not yours.

71. Analyze Your Solicitation Performance

Unless you're batting a thousand on all your solicitation calls, there's always room to improve your delivery.

Shortly after completing a call, assess your performance by answering these questions:

Did I...

... genuinely observe and listen to the prospect?

... speak with confidence?

... suggest a specific dollar amount?

... point out benefits of giving that were in line with the prospect's interests?

... place this prospect's long-term relationship with our organization over any short-term gains?

... fully convey impact the gift would have on the people we serve?

Was I able to fully answer the prospect's questions?

72. During Prospect Calls, Flexibility Is Key

Development professionals can get so wrapped up in gathering information prior to a prospect call that when it comes time to make the ask, they forget the two most important elements: listening to the donor and maintaining flexibility.

That's according to Marla Kaminsky, development associate, The Botsford Foundation (Farmington Hills, MI).

"I'm not saying something development professionals don't already know. It's just something we can all be reminded of from time to time," says Kaminsky. "It's important for us as fundraisers to be flexible with the donors and listen to what they are saying. Not only must we be prepared to talk about the agency's needs, but we also must be prepared to talk about the donors' wants and needs."

Kaminsky says she was reminded of this lesson during a prospect call at a previous job: "In the past, this donor had always made philanthropic gifts geared toward his profession (real estate) and I don't think he had ever shown interest in anything else. During our conversation he started talking about a new women's program for our organization."

The call resulted in two pledges on the spot to commit in excess of $10,000 for the program the meeting was initially set up for and for the program in which the donor also expressed interest.

"That call taught me to not always have the meeting mapped out in my head," Kaminsky says. "Now when I go into a prospect call, I have an idea of a specific outcome but am not married to it."

Source: Marla Kaminsky, Development Associate, The Botsford Foundation, Farmington Hills, MI. Phone (248) 442-5045. E-mail: mkaminsky@botsford.org

73. How to Sell What Donors Can't See

Intangible giving options, such as an endowment, are not always the easiest to sell to potential donors, yet they are often critical to the long-term future of an organization. So, how do you sell what your donors can't see or touch?

Aggie Sweeney, CEO, The Collins Group (Seattle, WA), shares three ways to help sell donors on intangible giving options:

1. Quantify and clearly articulate the outcomes possible as a result of their gift.

2. Be able to engage the donor in the organization's work (e.g., take them on a tour of your programs).

3. Talk about what will be lost if this philanthropic investment is not made (e.g., if a social service agency, talk about lives lost; if a heritage organization, talk about the history that will be unpreserved).

"Whatever you can do to offer tangible engagement in the organization can help the donor see the value in intangible giving," she says.

Sweeney shares an example of a youth organization with whom she worked that needed to raise significant endowment funds for an environmental education program: "They took the donor and the donor's family out to a camp location, where they experienced the diversity of the environment, the shoreline and the forest, as well as seeing students involved in environmental education. Endowment is by nature a long-term investment, and with this visit the family was able to experience firsthand how they would be able to help future students learn about environmental education. The family ended up making a naming gift and helping to endow and permanently preserve that camp so that it will be available for generations to come."

Your success as a professional fundraiser will depend, in part, on your ability to help people visualize what could be.

Source: Aggie Sweeney, CEO, The Collins Group, Seattle, WA. Phone (206) 728-1755. E-mail: aggies@collinsgroup.com

74. Use Principal Gifts To Leverage Key Groups

Whenever someone makes what you consider to be an extraordinary gift based on his/her position, age or professional standing, consider how you might use that gift as an example in leveraging similar gifts from others.

For instance, if a physician makes a $1.5 million commitment, it may make sense to use that example when approaching other physicians — assuming the donor has given you permission to do so.

75. When Is a Prospect Ready to Be Asked?

How do you know when it's time to ask for a major gift? Although several factors come into play, there are three primary criteria that should be taken into consideration.
They are:

1. The prospect's giving history — an indication of both capacity and proclivity to give.

2. The knowledge that sufficient cultivation has taken place.

3. Signals from the prospect that indicate now is the time.

76. Closing Techniques

- **The Written Close** — If you have properly led the prospect to the point of solicitation, you can sometimes begin walking through the paperwork associated with a gift and not even have to pose the question. Unless the prospect stops you, it's a done deal.

- **Bottom-up Method** — Help the prospect make decisions on matters subordinate to the pledge: type of gift, how it would be used, what the fund might be named, who and how many the gift would benefit, and so forth. Decisions on these matters help to visualize the gift and how it will look after it is made.

- **The Repetitive Yes Close** — This close builds a chain of yeses to questions the development officer asks to help lead the prospect into saying yes to the solicitation request. To put the customer in the habit of saying yes, ask questions you're sure will get affirmative answers.

- **Bracket Close** — Make three gift offers, the first being the largest — maybe even out of the prospect's range of giving; the second a more affordable but still a stretch gift; and the third a lower gift that has much less attractive benefits to the donor.

- **Bandwagon Close** — This closing technique emphasizes being a part of the enthusiasm associated with a fundraising effort: "Dr. Walters, I can't believe the sense of excitement people are showing for this campaign! I would really like you to join in this popular cause by making your pledge today."

78. Work at Improving Your Negotiation Skills

Knowing when and how to negotiate is both an art and a science. Many successful solicitations are the result of appropriately timed and thought-out negotiations.

Here are three techniques that can help you become a better negotiator:

1. Determine your position in advance of your appointment and anticipate the prospect's possible reactions so you will be prepared with counter offers.

2. Don't get so hung up on details that you lose sight of your primary objective. If, for instance, the prospect prefers to pay your requested amount over a five-year period rather than two years, be prepared to accept those conditions.

3. Pay attention to what is motivating the donor. It pays to listen. Be sensitive to what is motivating the potential gift, and use that information to close your sale. If the prospect is driven by ego, for instance, focus on those donor benefits.

77. What You Need to Know To Solicit Major Gifts

Q: "What key advice can you share about soliciting major gifts?"

"One challenge is balancing the university's strategic goals with donors' sights. This is difficult during post-campaign years, when the university is updating and revising its strategic plan. It's important for development officers to be aware of the university focus during the post-campaign period. Being proficient in conveying the university's process and updated plans early to prospective donors is a key to future fundraising success."

— Virginia C. Doud, Assistant Vice President for Major Gifts, Radford University Foundation, Inc. (Radford University, VA)

"Always try to meet prospective donors on your ground. I remember vividly what a prominent person said when we walked across a bare concrete slab, which was the floor of a new gymnasium. He said he wished he would have had a place like that to play when he was growing up. He caught the vision while standing on that concrete slab. It would have been more difficult to get to that point while sitting in his plush office overlooking the city."

— Bud Dickerson, Director of Major Gifts and Capital Campaigns, Fresno Pacific University (Fresno, CA)

"My approach has been to present a menu of expenses related to a project we're attempting to fund. I thought that an item from this display would intrigue the prospect in funding the project, and I would let them decide the gift level. I've learned that this menu approach can confuse them, as they are unclear on what we want. My new, more successful approach is to present the project budget and then clarify which project component and gift range we're hoping they will consider. This approach is specific and the subsequent dialogue has produced higher gift ranges."

— Kelly Ruggirello, President, Pacific Chorale, Santa Ana (Fresno, CA)

79. Tip for Overcoming Donor Objections

Difficult as it may feel, when a prospect makes an objection, try saying nothing for at least five seconds. The pause helps you to maintain control and allows you to gather your thoughts before responding. Equally important, by waiting for a brief period, the prospect may respond again and actually begin to overcome his/her own objection.

80. Common Errors in Soliciting Major Gifts

There are many pitfalls that organizations can encounter when attempting to raise major gifts. Here are three common mistakes:

Error: Not asking for a specific amount. It is often difficult for an inexperienced volunteer to comfortably articulate an ask for a very significant sum.
Solution: Props can be helpful. A scale of gifts chart that indicates how many gifts are required at each level allows the solicitor to simply point to the appropriate level and ask for support in this range.

> — *Lisa Barnwell Williams, Managing Partner,*
> *Skystone Ryan Inc. (Cincinnati, OH)*

Error: Not listening.
Solution: Instead of doing all the talking, ask questions that provide a chance for the potential donor to speak…and to speak from the heart. If you have done most of the talking in a solicitation, you have probably not listened to what the donor is really saying.

> — *Del Martin, Managing Partner and Chairman,*
> *Alexander Haas Martin and Partners (Atlanta, GA)*

Error: Failure to give the ask the deference it is due.
Solution: A request for a major gift — and the prospect from whom it is being requested — should be treated with the utmost respect. This means the request should be preceded with sufficient opportunity to interest and cultivate the prospective donor and that the ask is made in person in a setting where the prospect and solicitor clearly understand the purpose of the meeting.

> — *Jennifer Furla, Executive Vice President,*
> *Jeffrey Byrne and Associates, Inc. (Kansas City, MO)*

81. Team Solicitation Approach

Next time you're looking to make a significant ask, consider having a peer of the prospective donor try this:

"My wife (or husband) and I have pledged $100,000. We would like to have you join us at this level."

It's hard to beat having a current major donor put the question to a prospect you hope will give at that same level!

82. Demonstrate the Cumulative Impact of a Gift

As you approach the point of solicitation, it's helpful to show a prospect how a particular gift will impact your organization and those you serve over time. This is particularly useful with certain types of major gifts (e.g., endowment, programming and personnel).

You can illustrate the long-term impact of a gift as a portion of your written proposal or it can be shared as a stand-alone document. Referred to as a gift impact summary, this can also be used as a tool to help negotiate the exact terms of a particular gift. In the case of an endowed scholarship, for instance, the number of students to receive awards, the individual award amounts and other details can be finalized by using the summary as a starting point.

The gift impact summary also helps ensure both the donor and charity are on the same page with regard to details surrounding the actual gift (e.g., payment schedule, when the fund begins) and its eventual use (e.g., who benefits, how many, etc).

Two generic examples (shown at right) help illustrate the most basic types of information you might wish to include in your gift impact summary. Your actual summary would no doubt be lengthier and include more details.

Examples of Gift Impact Summaries

Named Endowed Scholarship
Gift Amount: $100,000
Anticipated Yearly Award (five percent): $5,000

Use of Gift: To provide annual scholarship awards to financially deserving women majoring in math or science.

Five-Year Results: 25 Cumulative Scholarship Awards at $1,000 each.

10-Year Results: 50 Cumulative Scholarship Awards at $1,000 each.

Domestic Violence Endowment
Gift Amount: $250,000
Anticipated Yearly Funds (five percent): $12,500

Use of Gift: To provide career assistance and job placement opportunities for adults seeking shelter at the agency by underwriting, in part, an employee position responsible for assisting clients with career development and job placement opportunities.

Five-Year Results: Based on past occupancy rates, career and job assistance will have been available to more than 1,000 deserving clients.

10-Year Results: Based on past occupancy rates, career and job assistance will have been available to more than 2,000 deserving clients.

83. Alter Cookie-cutter Approach When Soliciting Entrepreneurs

Does your development office have a plan to address the solicitation of entrepreneurs as major gift donors?

Because entrepreneurs don't function well in the typical bureaucratic process, Lisa Dietlin, president/CEO, Lisa M. Dietlin and Associates, Inc. (Chicago, IL), says it's important for nonprofits to alter the cookie-cutter approach that is used for corporate CEOs or donors.

Dietlin answers some questions about entrepreneurial giving:

How should a development officer approach an entrepreneur differently then a corporate CEO or donor?

"It is important to remember that entrepreneurs think outside the box. Unlike corporate CEOs who would consider funding something that others are already supporting, an entrepreneur will look at opportunities that no one has funded yet and be very intrigued and interested in supporting it. Development officers should keep this in mind; take new projects to entrepreneurs for support and community supported or existing projects to corporate CEOs for funding."

What can development officers do to solicit major gifts from entrepreneurs?

"Don't waste their time. For nonprofits, this means being prepared, make the interaction informative and above all, ensure the investment of the entrepreneur's time has worthwhile results moving them closer to committing the financial resources being sought. Entrepreneurs often show their frustration via their body language, so pay attention to the cues during any interaction. While entrepreneurs can multi-task, it is very easy to recognize they are becoming disengaged with the conversation. Also, know that if you are following a prescribed script, not allowing for flexibility, you will probably not be successful. They value flexibility and will want that in return in their interactions with you."

What should be kept in mind when approaching an entrepreneur for a major gift?

"First, entrepreneurs are risk takers. They love taking a chance with the potential of solving large problems. When engaged with a nonprofit, they will want and insist on doing this. They will want to roll up their sleeves and get the work done. Second, they are interested in addressing issues and causes, not supporting institutions. They will use market-based approaches to solve today's societal problems. They are attracted to addressing the root of the problem and ensuring the changes made possible are permanent. Finally, they expect a return on their investment. They are usually hands-on and want to guarantee that their donations are leveraged to the maximum possibility."

What advantages can come from soliciting an entrepreneur?

"The benefits are numerous but primarily the ability to transform one's organization. Entrepreneurs prefer to donate to new initiatives or solve current problems, all of which moves your organization and its programs to a different place."

Are there any disadvantages?

"Entrepreneurs are impatient. They dislike bureaucracy and paperwork, and are less likely to attend meetings or group activities. A development officer will have to be very creative and fast-paced to keep the process moving forward, ensuring a win-win outcome for both them and the organization."

Source: Lisa Dietlin, President/CEO, Lisa M. Dietlin and Associates, Inc., Chicago, IL. Phone (773) 772-4465. E-mail: lisa@lmdietlin.com

Skills to Form an Entrepreneurial Relationship

According to Lisa Dietlin, president/CEO, Lisa M. Dietlin and Associates, Inc. (Chicago, IL), a development officer must possess and employ these five skills when forming a relationship with an entrepreneur:

1. **Patience.** Entrepreneurs can take a long time to get to the point of making the decision, but know that once you get there, the process will go incredibly fast.

2. **Good sense of timing.** Time financial requests to an entrepreneur's business cycle. In other words, be aware of when they are cash rich or cash poor.

3. **Ability to push ahead quickly.** It is an essential skill for the development officer to be fast-paced, constantly expressing a sense of urgency to the entrepreneur. Remember, entrepreneurs like to be the first, fix a problem or identify something new that could be done.

4. **Diplomacy.** Entrepreneurs can be unrealistic in their expectations. Remember, it's the development officer's job to broker the unrealistic expectations with reality while trying to move programs forward and achieve goals.

5. **Open-mindedness.** Because entrepreneurs have unique problem-solving skills, it is the development officer's responsibility to be open-minded and at times an advocate for this new suggestion.

"Working with entrepreneurs is every bit worth the effort," says Dietlin. "Sometimes it can be like a roller coaster ride, with many ups and downs, twists and turns, and scary moments… but overall, it can result in an exhilarating experience that will produce transformational outcomes."

84. Sharpen Your Sales Skills

Your ability to convince major donors that your organization is worthy of their support is key to success, especially when competing with other charities for those same dollars. Keep these 10 principles in mind as you strengthen your sales skills:

1. **Know how to differentiate your product.** Distinguishing your organization from others that offer similar services is critical. What makes your nonprofit unique and sets it head-and-shoulders above the rest?

2. **Practice, practice, practice.** The more you push yourself into selling situations, the more proficient and successful you become.

3. **Recognize your organization's salable virtues.** Ask colleagues what they see as your organization's positive characteristics. What achievements, large and small, can you share with would-be donors?

4. **Share poignant examples of how your cause makes a difference in people's lives.** Draft a handful of real-life examples you can share over and over again with new audiences.

5. **Be passionate about your mission.** To effectively sell your mission, your enthusiasm must be contagious.

6. **Treat each call as the day's most important opportunity.** Don't view a call as a task that needs to be completed. Rather, know that this may be the most important action you will undertake today. Think of yourself as a dream broker.

7. **Be a sensitive listener.** Listen intently to would-be donors speak. What are they really saying? Be prepared to ask additional probing questions.

8. **Discover what motivates each probable donor to invest** (e.g., ego, altruism, affiliation). Build ask around that motivation.

9. **Learn to positively deal with rejection.** Look at each "no" as one step closer to the next "yes", realizing also that "no" may mean "not now".

10. **Be committed to appropriate follow-up.** Every meeting should result in some form of follow-up. Keep building on each relationship.

85. Solicitation Advice

- **Close with confidence.** Once you start to ask for a gift, don't back off. Speak with confidence. Stay relaxed. Don't vary the tone or pace of your voice. If you do, the prospect may sense your tension and hesitate to contribute.

- **Role-play solicitation.** Prior to making a solicitation call, especially if two or more people are involved, practice asking for the gift. Speaking words out loud and hearing how they sound will help you shape and refine your request for support.

- **Rather than getting a prospect to think about an amount of money to give, get him/her to think about funding a particular project.**

- **Recognize that receiving a "no" to a solicitation call may simply mean "not now".** The individual may, in fact, be telling you: "I don't want you to give up on me; I just don't want to commit at this time."

- **If you find yourself hesitant to suggest a specific amount when setting the stage for a major gift request, use a chart that identifies levels of major gifts.** Refer to the chart and tell the prospect, "Picture yourself among this group of donors." By giving the prospect a level rather than an amount, you can set out to negotiate a major gift commitment.

86. Team Solicitation Tip

- When making a team solicitation, know in advance who will be making the ask and be sure the other individual knows to remain silent until the prospect fully responds or is signaled by the solicitor to speak.

87. Find the Right Word

When speaking with or writing to a would-be donor, consider your choice of words and phrases:

✓ Instead of contribute, say invest.

✓ Rather than asking for a gift, extend an invitation: "I would like to invite you to invest $250,000 in this critical effort."

✓ Go beyond saying "your gift will make a difference" to demonstrate impact: "Your gift will enable us to conduct far more detailed research in the fight against cancer."

✓ Be confident and specific with the messages you convey. Rather than saying "Would you consider increasing your gift?" explain the importance of increased giving: "A 20 percent increase will allow us to keep pace with..."

88. 30-day Contact Plan Helps Firm Up Objectives

It's easy for other stuff to consume a work day, and before you know it, a week has come and gone and little attention has been given to what matters most: meaningful contact with prospects and donors.

To help stay focused on making contacts, outline a 30-day plan each month. Decide who it is you most need to contact — and why — then set out to make appointments

and complete correspondence/phone calls in advance. A contact plan form (such as the example shown below) helps to visualize what lies ahead. It doesn't mean plans can't be changed, but does help ensure accountability for making prospect/donor contacts on a regular basis. The plan also forces you to use your limited time to prioritize who among your prospect/donor pool you most need to contact.

30-day Contact Plan

Development Officer _____ Month Of _____

Primary Contacts

Name	Prospect/ Donor	Objective	Target Amount	Comments

Secondary Contacts (If Time Permits)

Name	Prospect/ Donor	Objective	Target Amount	Comments

89. Highlight Impact of Funding to Distinguish Your Organization From the Pack

When submitting a funding proposal, particularly to an individual, be sure to spell out the impact the gift could have in distinguishing your organization from others. How would this gift put your organization on the map? What could it do to help build your organization's regional, statewide or national reputation?

While most donors are interested in knowing the impact of their gifts on persons served by the organization (e.g., students, patients, youth), many are also motivated by allegiance to the organization itself. Many donors want to know their major gifts are elevating the charity's standing among similar types of nonprofits.

Distinguishing Language Examples

When describing the impact of a major gift in your proposal, go beyond the direct impact on those you serve to point out how the gift will help your organization's public standing. These examples show how a major gift might help distinguish one nonprofit from other competing organizations:

✓ The acquisition of this piece of equipment will elevate [name of medical facility] into the top 10 percent of the nation's cancer centers.

✓ The successful completion of this capital campaign will make our school among the most highly endowed institutions in the state of Ohio.

✓ This gift, which would be the largest in the history of our organization, will impact every corner of the state, making [name of organization] among the most highly regarded museums in this part of the nation.

90. Use Smaller Projects To Cement a Relationship

It happens often: You discover someone with significant financial capability, even interests in line with your nonprofit's mission, but with no real connection to your charity.

What steps can you take to turn those ideal factors into a transformational gift?

Rather than starting a long, drawn-out relationship-building plan with the hope of landing a seven-figure gift, consider inviting the prospect to fund a smaller but highly visible project as a way to jump-start the relationship.

One hospital asked a couple to fund a $20,000 fountain on its grounds as a way to establish an immediate relationship. The couple agreed, and hospital officials held a public dedication with the couple present when the fountain was completed. That occasion cemented a relationship with the couple who previously had no ties to the hospital, and 14 months later they made another gift — for millions of dollars.

91. Re-approach Those Who Said 'No' in Past

Hearing "no" from a prospect may simply mean "not now". Timing is crucial.

Here are some techniques to use when approaching prospects who declined your solicitation in the past:

✓ Evaluate why your first request was rejected, then arm yourself with new information.

✓ Select a new funding opportunity.

✓ Take a new team solicitor along.

✓ Cite contribution examples of respected colleagues.

✓ Ask for a smaller amount to get the donor on board.

✓ For corporate/business asks, determine if there is someone else in the firm who also has decision-making authority.

92. Respect the Power of Listening

Major gift fundraising is more about listening than talking. In fact, solicitors who talk too much tend to fail, says Andy Robinson (Plainfield, VT), trainer, consultant and author of "Big Gifts for Small Groups" (Emerson & Church).

"Novices are the worst offenders because they're filled with nervous energy," says Robinson. Uncomfortable with silence, they "work doubly hard to carry the conversation. They mistakenly believe that... armed with the perfect case, they can talk somebody into giving, so they obsess about getting the language right."

He says development officers can actually talk people out of giving. To prevent that from happening, listen someone into giving by asking good questions and being fully present in the conversation. He points to fundraising guru Jerold Panas who calls this "listening the gift."

"Fundraising isn't about money — it's about relationships," says Robinson. "How do you feel when friends or family talk too much and monopolize the conversation? Or when they get excited about their interests and passions and problems, but never ask about yours? Would you rather listen to a monologue or join a dialogue?"

He advises asking these questions when meeting with donors or prospects:

- Why are you interested in our work?

- What is your experience with our issue? Has someone you know been affected?

- (For current donors): Last year, you gave $___. Why did you do it? What is it about our work that moves you?

- What are your favorite causes? Why?

- When you make a donation, how do you like to be acknowledged?

"Remember, your job is to stimulate dialogue, and the best way to do that is to ask questions," says Robinson. "People like to talk about themselves, so make it easy. The more they talk, the better your chance of getting the gift — not because you manipulate them, but because you're genuinely interested in their point of view. If you know what motivates them, you'll be a more responsive partner."

Source: Andy Robinson, Trainer, Consultant and Author, Plainfield, VT. Phone (802) 479-7365. E-mail: andyfund@earthlink.net

93. Who Should Make Up The Solicitation Team?

It's important to put some thought into who should make up your solicitation team for each major gift call. A development officer? The CEO? A board member or volunteer, or some combination thereof?

More often than not, a solicitation team comprised of two individuals — a staff person and a significant other — makes for an ideal approach. Or in some instances it might make more sense to have two staff members: one to solicit the gift and the other to address any technical questions.

Whatever combination you choose for each call, decide in advance who will do the asking and negotiating, and who will play the support role. And recognize that the support role is equally as important as that of the solicitor.

94. Tailor Presentations to Individuals' Interests

Learning to tailor individual presentations to would-be donors' interests is a craft that requires thorough prospect research and sensitive listening skills. That's why knowing as much as possible about prospects' interests prior to the solicitation is so important.

Sometimes prospects' interests will have a direct link to funding projects while at other times the relationship will be more abstract.

Whether through cultivation visits prior to solicitation or other research efforts, work to garner information to help identify your prospects' interests and shape your solicitation. Below are some categories to help you learn more about prospects:

Interest Categories, Key Facts

Here are some interest categories and important information that may be helpful to know about your major gift prospects:

Personal Interests
- Importance placed on family
- Leisure-time activities
- What matters most in life
- Importance placed on education
- Financial philosophy
- Philanthropic interests
- Civic involvement/interests
- Future hopes and plans
- Close friends
- Pet peeves
- Personal heroes
- Religious preference/importance

Political Persuasion
- Conservative versus liberal
- Passive versus strong opinions
- Opinions on social issues

Business/Career
- Career progression
- Current responsibilities
- Accomplishments and setbacks
- Business connections
- Management style
- Community, statewide and/or national involvement

95. Identify Your Prospects' Response Motivators

What causes people to contribute to various causes? What motivates their gifts?

Response motivators are complex. The pathway leading from the "guttural" mechanism to an individual's choice of response is different for every person, depending on that individual's own life experiences. Yet, humans respond to a set of common psychological factors.

Knowledge of these response motivators can aid fundraising efforts and positively reinforce donors in their decision to contribute.

Some examples of response motivators include, but are not limited to:

- **The ego factor** — All people seek attention and have the need to be recognized. Never underestimate the stroking power of named gifts, awards, special attention from your CEO and more.

- **The altruistic spirit** — Some individuals contribute purely for altruistic reasons, among the most noble of all. Donors among this group sometimes prefer to remain anonymous.

- **The desire for immortality** — Leaving a legacy becomes more important as we age. We look for ways to validate our existence and be remembered.

- **The need for safety** — Safety and security are essential for mental health. People need to feel they and those they care about are safe and secure. The missions of many nonprofits address these issues.

- **The need to belong** — Humans are social animals. Our identities are, in part, a result of the groups to which we belong with everyone aiming for connections of varying sorts.

96. Be Careful Not to Overclose

When making the ask, be mindful of not overstating your case. A solicitor who goes on and on making the case for support runs the risk of talking the donor out of a gift. This tendency to say more than is needed is sometimes based on the fear that the prospect will say no.

Accept that a prospect's decision to give or not give is not a personal reflection on you. Instead, know how you plan to word your ask before meeting with the prospect, then ask and remain silent until he/she has fully responded to your request.

97. Face Call Anxiety Head On

It's commonplace to have a bit of nervousness prior to a prospect call. In fact, a little apprehension is healthy — it keeps us on our toes. But if nervousness is impeding our delivery, something needs to be done. Recognizing call anxiety and accepting it is half the battle.

Before making a prospect call, ask yourself what's the worst that can happen. Rejection, right? Well, rejection goes with the territory. You can handle it. So not to worry. Now get on with that call!

98. Expert Advice Will Help You Turn Donor Objections Into Gift Opportunities

Before you can turn donor objections into opportunities, you must first realize one key concept, according to Sandra Ehrlich, director of fund development services, and Dawn M.S. Miller, senior consultant, Zielinksi Companies (St. Louis, MO): Fundraising is sharing what you believe in such a way that you offer your donors an opportunity to participate with you in your mission, core values and vision.

"A donor objection is truly a window of opportunity for the solicitor to listen and draw the donor closer to his or her mission," says Ehrlich. "Giving is based on the wants and needs of the donor. Therefore, your role is to help the donor visualize the end result the gift will make to the greater community by overcoming their objections."

Studies show the oral presentation is ultimately what motivates donors to make the gift, the fundraising experts say. Through philanthropic storytelling, you inspire and motivate donors by sharing the urgency, importance and relevance of their gifts.

"When soliciting major gifts one-on-one, it is vital to listen and watch for those nonverbal cues and clues that make up roughly 85 percent of the conversation," says Miller. "At the same time, listen for 'gifting noises' and donor objections that demonstrate how deeply the donor cares about your mission."

Before a solicitation meeting, they advise, role-play situations and ask a series of questions to uncover and overcome objections. Remember to restate donor questions and objections, and identify when the donor is listening or he/she is shutting down.

"Hank Rosso, founder of The Fundraising School in San Francisco, said that there are six right considerations in the gift solicitation process to maximize fundraising success," says Miller. "They are: the right person asks the right prospect for the right amount of money for the right cause at the right time and in the right way."

To overcome objections, say Ehrlich and Miller, you will need to objectively listen for and determine the answers to these six key questions:

1. Am I the right solicitor, or natural partner, for this donor?
2. Is this a philanthropic fit for the donor? Is this one of his/her top three priorities?
3. Is it the amount we're asking?
4. Is it the organization? The project? The program? Is it who we are serving?
5. Is it the right time for the donor to make a gift of this magnitude?
6. What would the donor like to support? How would the donor like to make the gift?

"By closely examining what the donor is saying, and perhaps more importantly, not saying, you can turn the donor's objections into a gift," says Ehrlich.

Sources: Sandra G. Ehrlich, Director of Fund Development Services, and Dawn M.S. Miller, Senior Consultant, Zielinski Companies, St. Louis, MO. Phone (800) 489-2150; (314) 644-2150. E-mail: sehrlich@zielinskico.com or dmiller@zielinskico.com

Additional Techniques Help Turn Objections Into Gifts

Turn donor objections into gifts by listening without interrupting to hear the real objection, say Sandra Ehrlich, director of fund development services, and Dawn M.S. Miller, senior consultant, Zielinkski Companies (St. Louis, MO). Additional advice from the fundraising experts on how to turn donor objections into gifts:

- Empathize.
- If it's a money issue, offer alternative methods/time frames for making payments.
- Use "and" rather than "but" statements and stay positive and encouraging.
- Offer additional information or opportunities such as, "Would you like to meet with XYZ to hear first-hand to see how your gift will impact ABC?"
- Schedule another meeting. Many people take more time to make a large financial decision and will want to consult with close and trusted advisors.

Be Prepared to Answer Common Gift Objections

Don't take no for an answer when soliciting a donor for a major gift. Sandra Ehrlich, director of fund development services, and Dawn M.S. Miller, senior consultant, Zielinski Companies (St. Louis, MO), share their answers to 10 common donor gift objections:

1. The donor says: "I just don't know." You say: "What are your concerns?"
2. The donor says: "I can't make up my mind." You say: "What have I left unclear?"
3. The donor says: "I'm not ready to give." You say: "When would be a good time?"
4. The donor says: "No." You say: "May I ask why?" (Remember, "no" is not usually forever — is "no" right now?)
5. The donor says: "Your request is too high." You say: "In respect to what?"
6. The donor says: "I'd like to help, but that figure is way out of my range." You say: "What would you feel comfortable giving at this time?"
7. The donor says: "I don't have enough money." Or, "I'm going to retire in a few years." You say: "What if I can show you a way to make a gift?"
8. The donor says: "I have to talk to my husband/wife first." You say: "When would it be convenient for us to talk together?"
9. The donor says: "I need to make sure my spouse is provided for." You say: "What if we talk about gift plans that may help you provide income for your spouse and support our organization too?"
10. The donor says: "I don't give lump sums." Or, "I don't make pledges." You say: "How would you prefer to give?" or "What would work better for you?"

99. Presentation Tools for Face-to-face Calls

Artists' renderings of a new building or renovation and similar presentation tools are effective ways to help donors visualize a project during a face-to-face presentation.

Beth Nelson, director of major gifts, Lafayette College (Easton, PA), says she uses presentation tools during solicitation calls, but judiciously: "I like to tell the story first and build the emotional and positive aspects of making a gift. I then use the presentation tools when I want to foster visualization of the project. I won't do so, however, if I think the donor will be distracted and not listen to the story."

When making a presentation for a capital project, Nelson brings artistic renderings and/or floor plans. For a renovation project, she will also bring current floor plans to show what the building could become. For a programmatic project, she will bring brochures and pamphlets to show the existing program and what proper funding could add to it.

"I will also sometimes draft a brochure that illustrates what the potential program, if funded, would look like," she says. "If I were soliciting funding for an endowed lecture series, for example, I might bring along the materials for an existing lecture series to show what could be possible for the new one."

Nelson has also used a gift table during face-to-face major gift presentations to illustrate to lead donors where they fit in the campaign.

She cautions against using presentation tools with too much text: "If you do, don't pull them out until the end of the presentation, or donors will start reading and stop listening to you."

The only other presentation materials Nelson has at face-to-face calls are what she refers to as "logistical materials" needed to close a major gift, such as a deed of gift or gift agreement, either already drafted with donor information included, or as a sample with information needed highlighted. "I would not bring these materials out at a solicitation, however, unless the donor indicates he or she is ready for that step," she says. "Instead, I would mail them to the donor after I have sent a thank-you note."

Source: Elizabeth Nelson, Director of Major Gifts, Lafayette College, Easton, PA. Phone (610) 330-5839.

100. Science of Asking Questions

■ When meeting with a prospect for purposes of information gathering, it's not enough simply to ask probing questions. Arrange your questions sequentially, beginning with those that are more generalized and moving toward more specific ones.

102. Offer Businesses Choices for Giving

When calling on a business, especially one that has no prior involvement with your nonprofit, don't simply ask for a gift. Go beyond to offer a menu of options that may result in multiple types of gifts. Here's a proposed script to get you started.

Development Officer: "In addition to telling you more about our agency and its programs, I want to share some ways your business can really help us make a difference in the lives of those we serve. Specifically, I want to invite you to consider four types of involvement: 1) sponsoring one of many programs or events; 2) making an outright gift that would support our organization's work; 3) exploring gifts-in-kind; or 4) partnering with us on a program of mutual interest."

Offering multiple options gives the business an opportunity to choose those it considers most attractive. It's more difficult to say no to choices than a simple request for a gift. And who knows, some businesses may choose all four options.

101. Swim With Solicitation Pros Who Know How to Ask

New to the development profession? Or could your solicitation skills perhaps use a bit of refining?

To polish your solicitation skills and learn more about the art of asking, spend time with those who have a track record of success. Identify two or three seasoned professionals and:

1. **Get them to talk about their fundraising style.** How do they know what to say and when to say it? Do they have some standard lines from which to choose?

2. **Watch them in action.** If you work for the same nonprofit, ask to accompany them on some calls to observe them in action.

3. **Invite them to critique you.** Whether you do some role playing or they accompany you on some calls to observe your style, ask for honest feedback on specific ways you can improve your approach.

103. Solicitation Procedures

■ If your prospect relies on someone else for financial advice, that person should be present during your solicitation.

■ Before leaving a solicitation meeting, be sure you clearly understand how the donor intends to make the gift.

104. Plan Ahead: Solicitation Strategies Worksheet

Going to ask for a major gift? Plan ahead by using this two-person solicitation strategies worksheet.

"It provides structure for people, so one doesn't dominate the conversation and so the process is thought out," says Jim Lewis, partner, Lewis Kennedy Associates (Portland, OR). "While one is conducting the conversation, the other can observe body language and listen."

The worksheet helps you outline who will say what, what the possible questions or objections might be and who will ask for the gift. "It forces some planning by people, so they just don't go out and wing it — which can be a

disaster because in the middle of the conversation you may find out that one person doesn't really know the mission of the organization or why they are there," says Lewis.

Also, other than to provide structure, Lewis says, "It's designed to remove as much as possible the fear of gift asking." Being prepared and knowing the plan of action can not only eliminate any apprehensions, but can help make the ask go smoother, which may result in the desired gift.

Source: Jim Lewis, Partner, Lewis Kennedy Associates, Portland, OR. Phone (503) 236-4850, ext. 202. E-mail: jim@lewiskennedy.com

Content not available in this edition

105. Prepare, Practice to Better Handle Donor Objections

Before you make that all-important face-to-face ask of a major donor, be sure you do your homework to ensure that the donor is both willing to support the project and capable of making a gift in the amount of your ask, says John H. Taylor, associate vice chancellor of advancement services, North Carolina State University (Raleigh, NC).

"The number of donor objections will be low if you've done your homework," says Taylor, "including researching the donor's giving history to your and similar organizations, and matching the donor's interests with your needs."

Objections do happen, however, even with the most careful research and cultivation of a donor. The fundraising expert shares some of the situations in which a donor might object to making a major gift and how to handle those objections:

"My financial situation has changed."

If you have not met with the donor for some time, you may not be aware of a change in the donor's financial situation. If the donor tells you that his or her financial situation has changed, the best and most appropriate response is to talk about payment options. For example, you can say that you are not talking about the donor making a $1 million gift today, but instead making a gift of $250,000 a year over a period of four years. If the donor still objects, you may have to put it on the back burner and come back to the donor at a later date.

"That project doesn't interest me."

This objection shouldn't happen very often if you have done your research, but in case you've picked the wrong project for the donor, you should always go into the solicitation with multiple gift options. "Although you will want to go in with a primary focus, you don't want to go in with only one choice or you will either have to go back to them later with a revised project, or fumble around with other ideas in

front of the donor," he says. "It's better to go in with two to three viable options and let the donor pick the one of greatest interest to him or her."

"Something happened at your organization recently that I'm not happy with."

You may have made the solicitation appointment six months ago, and in the interim, something has happened at your organization that has made your donor mad. "For example, your organization may have had some negative publicity that affected the donor's personal beliefs," Taylor says. "You will want to look introspectively at what has gone on at your organization between the time you made the appointment and the time of the solicitation to make sure nothing has happened. If it has, and you think your donor might be offended, you might want to reschedule your solicitation appointment until you can work out the problem with your donor."

Source: John H. Taylor, Associate Vice Chancellor, Advancement Services, North Carolina State University, Raleigh, NC. Phone (919) 513-2954. E-mail: johnhtaylor@ncsu.edu

106. Closing Questions

It's helpful to have a tool chest of closing phrases and questions from which to choose. Here are two to add to your selection:

"Are you leaning more toward an endowed scholarship at this point?" — Assumes a gift is forthcoming.

"With a scholarship of this size, you could assist four students each year for generations to come." — Helps the prospect visualize a gift in action.

107. Fresh Techniques to Add to Solicitation Repertoire

Does gift solicitation turn into a routine? Don't let it by using one or more of these techniques to solicit your next gift.

- **Keep in contact with development colleagues.** View colleagues in the fund development arena as partners striving for a common goal. Share ideas, discuss prospects and consider mutually beneficial joint development efforts. These relationships will both help on the revenue side and create positive public relations for all involved.

- **Send donors a complete report on how their gifts were spent and how they met a real need.** Donors will appreciate knowing you care enough about their gift (no matter its size) to keep them informed about how it was used and will likely remember this gesture next time you ask for a gift.

- **Research, research, research.** With today's easily accessible resources, do your homework before meeting with a prospective donor. Get to know as much as possible about them (e.g., education, profession, hobbies, giving habits, family, etc.) to best match the idea or funding opportunity with their interests. Determine what kind of givers they are (e.g., A prove-it's-important/statistical giver? Emotional giver? What's-in-it-for-me giver?) Then approach them from their need or perspective.

- **Personalize presentations.** Nothing turns off donors like a canned sales pitch. Do your homework and personalize solicitations to focus on why donors are special to you.

108. Individual Gift Proposals Vary Greatly

A gift proposal for an individual differs greatly from a proposal for a corporate or foundation donor in that it does not follow specific guidelines or require detailed information such as a budget for a campaign or project, says Vince Fraumeni, founder, V.J. Fraumeni Fundraising Consultants (Hacienda Heights, CA).

Individual gift proposals, Fraumeni says, "are also rarely going to be sent to cold donor prospects, but rather to specifically targeted individuals who either have a relationship with the organization or with an individual closely aligned with the organization, such as a board member or campaign committee member."

Many times an individual gift proposal will be sent at the individual's request, he says. "A prospect may ask to be sent more information about a project, or if they have a private foundation, may ask that a request for funds be sent to the foundation."

Gifts made by individuals through a private foundation, he says, are often made on a pre-selected basis, and the person will only accept proposals he/she has solicited.

Unlike a corporate or foundation gift proposal, which is normally done in the form of an application sometimes found on the corporation or foundation's website, an individual gift proposal is typically in the form of a letter, says Fraumeni.

The letter may only be one- to two-and-a-half pages, depending on the nature and scope of the campaign, he says. "A request for a larger gift in the six- to seven-figure range for a major institution such as a children's hospital or university could be a bit longer... (and) have more detail about the wide-ranging impact the gift will have on the community and those who will benefit from the completed project."

The first paragraph should thank the donor for the opportunity to submit the proposal and state the letter's purpose. It should include the specific dollar amount requested and what project those funds will support. That first paragraph should also include the total amount of the campaign goal so that the donor can see how his or her gift fits into the total campaign.

"Subsequent paragraphs of the letter should include information on what the project entails, the time line for beginning and completing the project or campaign, and how the project or campaign will impact the people you serve," he says.

The tone of the letter should be somewhere between formal and informal, yet be respectful and courteous and not presumptuous, says Fraumeni.

The letter should be signed by the most recognizable and/or senior person at your organization, he says, such as the president or CEO, board chair or campaign chair. "The letter should convey to the donor the impression that their role in the project or campaign is so important that the CEO is taking the time to write the letter," says Fraumeni. He notes the letter should be sent within a week of the donor's request for a proposal.

Source: Vincent J. Fraumeni, Founder/Principal, V.J. Fraumeni Fundraising Consultants, Hacienda Heights, CA. Phone (626) 369-1969. E-mail: vince@fraumeni.com

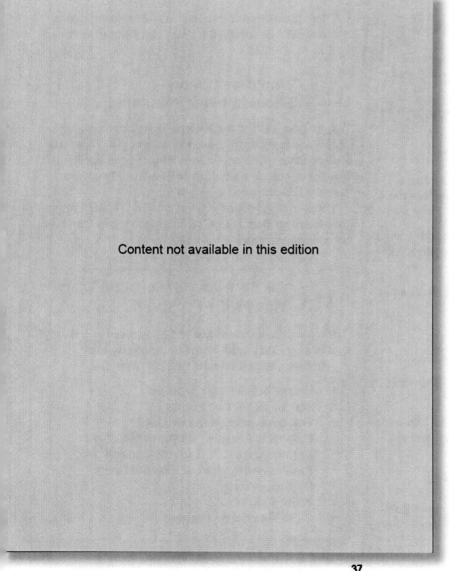

Content not available in this edition

This letter (names of the individuals have been changed) was sent to a donor prospect who did not have a relationship with the church organization requesting a major campaign gift but was closely tied to a church member who had died a year earlier. The church member, who was the prospect's youth pastor, had been instrumental in encouraging the prospect to be the first member of his family to attend college. The pastor, his wife and the donor prospect kept in touch throughout their lives. Although the prospect and pastor did not attend the same church, they were members of the same church organization. When the pastor died, the church sent the donor prospect a letter asking him to make a leadership gift to the campaign in memory of his beloved pastor and in honor of the pastor's wife. The donor said yes.

109. Incorporate 'Analogies' Into One-on-one Meetings

There are various sales tools and techniques you can use when meeting with would-be donors. One tool is the analogy — using a particular topic to make similar comparisons.

Before meeting with a prospect, consider their occupation, position and interests to prepare one or more analogies that will help make important points. To illustrate, let's say you represent a college or university and you're about to meet with the head of a manufacturing company. To underscore your institution's need for broad-based support, you might point out the importance of having a diverse customer base for their manufactured products.

Analogies can offer a springboard for further discussion and help prospects more fully relate to the challenges and needs of your organization.

111. Strike While You're Hot

Got some prospects you dread calling on for one reason or another? Try this: Whenever you close a gift you feel great about, go see that difficult prospect. There's no better time to do it than when you're feeling on top of your game.

112. Hone Your Listening Skills

Good listening habits are crucial to major gifts success. That's why you should consciously strive to improve those skills over time. To help do that:

✓ **Remember the 70/30 rule:** Get your prospects speaking 70 percent or more of the time, leaving 30 percent or less speaking time for you.

✓ **Echo key comments.** If you want further clarification on a particular point, repeat what was said.

114. Tips for Making the Ask

- Be specific in asking for a dollar amount. If possible, avoid presenting a gift range.

- Present the prospect with a written proposal. This makes it clear that your request is formal and implies that a formal response is needed.

- Strive to be diplomatic in making a major gift solicitation. Give your probable donor room to maneuver with wording such as this: "Susan, to fully fund this project, it will take $250,000. We invite you to consider a gift in that amount."

110. Two-member Team Is Ideal (In Most Cases)

How many individuals should be involved in making a solicitation call? The answer to that obviously depends on the circumstances, taking into account the amount requested, the would-be donor's personality and preferences, the proposed use of the gift and more.

Having said that, a two-member solicitation team may be ideal in most instances. As compared to one solicitor, a two-member team has the following advantages:

✓ Team members can complement one another, assuming two different roles. One may answer technical questions about the funding project while the other may serve as the key solicitor. Or one may be the prospect's peer while the other serves as solicitor.

✓ The power of listening, remembering, making observations and more is greater than that of one solicitor only.

✓ One team member can jump into the conversation to redirect it or support the other team member as needed.

113. Would-be Donors Shouldn't Feel Pressured

Bottom line: It's vital that a donor feels good about their decision to make a gift, especially a major gift. That's why it's important while you do everything to point out the benefits of making a gift that you do nothing to make a prospect feel pressured or obligated.

Remember, a donor who has decided to make a major investment on their own will remain a long-term friend and investor in your charity.

115. Be Sure Your Solicitation Team Knows the Prospect

If more than one individual will be involved in soliciting a major gift, be sure everyone on your solicitation team is familiar with the prospect's:

- Interest in this particular project
- Past giving to your organization
- Past involvement with your charity
- Philanthropic support of other organizations
- Business and personal accomplishments
- Family (spouse, children, extended family)
- Hobbies, interests
- Political views
- Close friends and associates

116. Overcoming Objections

- Whenever you get turned down for a gift, take a moment to analyze those feelings. Are you angry? Depressed? By consciously examining your state of mind following a rejection, you can more readily accept the experience, put it behind you and move on to an eventual success.

- Use a portion of regularly scheduled staff meetings to address possible donor objections and how to overcome them.

    Select an example of one donor objection for each meeting and then spend a few minutes discussing how to address or overcome that objection. Doing this will give each development officer greater confidence as she/he meets with would-be donors.

119. Solicitation Wording

It helps to be prepared with wording options as you walk through the solicitation process with donors. Here is one wording example that addresses maximizing the size of a donor's pledge:

"If it would help you give even more generously by spreading the payments over a two- or three-year period, we certainly welcome that option."

117. What's a Reasonable Ask?

When going to a new prospect for a first-time gift, how much should you ask for? If you can determine the prospect's favorite charity and learn how much he/she gives to that organization, you'll have one indication of what might amount to a reasonable request.

118. Closing Procedures

- After requesting a gift commitment from a prospect, never leave a blank pledge form without knowing the amount. Doing so will often result in a lower-than-hoped-for pledge.

120. Proposal Tips

- Include brief testimonials from other major donors in printed proposals. In addition to the positive impact it will have on the prospect, the testimonial will also strengthen ties with those donors who offered them.

121. Take Time to Evaluate Gift Refusals

As much as you need to pick yourself up and move on whenever your request for a gift is rejected, it's also important to determine what went wrong. By doing so, you can help increase your chances for success in the future.

Was it a matter of the wrong person doing the asking? Was the ask amount too far out of line? Was timing the issue?

Once the prospect has made a decision to give or not to give, don't be hesitant about asking a question or two that may help get at answers: "May I ask, could your decision be based

on timing? Could your circumstances be different in, say, six months?" Simply raising a probing question will probably begin to give you some useful evaluative information.

In addition to recording your conclusions in a call report, make use of a completed solicitations report that lists all of the asks you have made over a specified period of time — a month or a quarter, for example. Make entries to the report each time you finalize a closing call. Be as honest as possible in assessing why you were rejected.

Monthly Completed Solicitations Report				
Completed by _____			For period ending _____	
DATE	PROSPECT	PLEDGE/REFUSAL	AMOUNT REQUESTED	REASON FOR PLEDGE/REFUSAL

122. Plan for Success With Business Prospects

What are you doing to maximize success when it comes to soliciting support from the business community? Whether you use a particular prospect management software or a form such as the example shown here, your time and ultimate success will be best used by planning and prioritizing anticipated calls on businesses.

The process of identifying key players, discovering a company's recent history of giving, determining any existing links to your organization and more, will increase your odds for success as you map out a plan of research, cultivation and solicitation.

You might even consider forming a business advisory council made up of volunteers familiar with your business community to review names and make calls on businesses capable of making generous gifts. A form similar to this would be helpful in providing ongoing direction to your most capable volunteers.

Business Prospect Profile & Anticipated Moves Schedule

Name of Business _____

Address _____

City _____ State _____ ZIP _____

Company Contacts	Titles	Phone

Known Gift Recipients	Appr. Date	Gift Use

Matching gift company?   ☐ Yes   ☐ No
Published gift/grant guidelines?   ☐ Yes   ☐ No
Formal gifts committee/process?   ☐ Yes   ☐ No

Links to our organization:
1. _____ 3. _____
2. _____ 4. _____

Likely gift/sponsorship opportunities based on what we know today:
1. _____ 3. _____
2. _____ 4. _____

Anticipated plan for introduction:

Who	When	Objective

Anticipated cultivation moves:

When	What	By Whom

Target amount: $ _____

Anticipated solicitation:

When	Gift Use	By Whom

123. To Sell More Effectively, Know Your Product

A sound understanding of your nonprofit's product(s) — services and programs — is indispensable as you sell to would-be donors. Sales skills have little meaning without the ability to understand and explain your products to others.

Additionally, the more you can distinguish your products from the competition, the more passionate you become about the value of your nonprofit. And if you're enthused, others will more readily become enthused as well.

Make a habit to keep broadening knowledge of your nonprofit and its products.

To help do that:

1. **Pretend you're a prospect being introduced to an organization for the first time.** What questions might you have? What questions would you want answered if you were asked to make a sizable contribution? Write down the first 10 or 20 questions that come to mind and see if you can answer them. If not, learn the answers and script yourself to answer them properly and thoroughly.

2. **Begin a facts file to which you can add from time to time.** Whenever you discover a new piece of information about your place of employment, jot it down and include it in your facts file.

3. **Make time to regularly visit one on one with your nonprofit's employees.** Ask them questions about their work. Their insight will provide you with valuable knowledge.

4. **Keep comparing key facts about your nonprofit with the competition.** It helps to know where you're ahead and behind of the competition.

124. Sales Pitch Tip

■ When preparing prospect presentations, always remember their favorite radio station: WIIFM — "What's In It For Me?" Be mindful of that as you develop your sales pitch.

125. Team Solicitation Tip

■ When more than one person is involved in a solicitation call, plan your exit. Agree on when to conclude the conversation and be on your way.

126. Avoid Written Donor Details

Q: "How much major donor prospect information should you share with volunteer solicitors?"

Share very little personal or financial information about major donor prospects in writing with volunteer solicitors beyond the prospect's (and spouse's/partner's) name and full contact information, relationship with your organization and date by which the solicitation should be completed, advises Renata J. Rafferty, principal, Rafferty Consulting Group (Indian Wells, CA).

"I'm very hesitant to share details about prospects in writing with volunteers," Rafferty says. "I can't tell you how many times a written document, or the information on it, has unintentionally ended up in the hands of the prospect or donor. Nine times out of 10 they find it offensive. Or the solicitor's spouse sees it and either lets the information slip to others, or the information is used for some other non-related purpose (e.g., negotiating a business deal or targeting donor for another charity)."

Instead, she says, once you and/or the steering commit-tee review names of top prospects and determine who will solicit them, conduct a brief private session with the solicitor to discuss strategy for each prospect.

In this meeting, openly share with the solicitor information (financial and personal) relevant with respect to this particular prospect, she says. "They can take notes if they wish, and then you can decide together on the specific tack to be taken with the prospect. Presumably, your top prospects will be solicited by someone who already knows the prospect well or has some substantial connection to the prospect, so you'll know what's appropriate to share in each individual case."

Do not provide volunteers with written information such as amounts of past or current giving, target solicitation amount, etc., or personal information about interests, giving habits, net worth, etc., Rafferty says. "You can discuss all that in the private meeting, but do not let that circulate on an organization-generated document."

— Renata J. Rafferty, Principal,
Rafferty Consulting Group (Indian Wells, CA)

127. How to Respond to 'I'm Too Busy to Meet'

You phone a prospect to set up an appointment and get an immediate response: "I'm too busy to meet." It's an all-too-frequent obstacle to overcome. So how do you respond?

Here are three comebacks from which to choose:

• "I'm willing to meet any hour of any day that works for you, and I promise not to stay longer than 20 minutes unless you want me to. Is there a date and time that works best for you?"

• "I respect both your position and your time. Would it be possible for me to speak with your assistant to find a day and time that works best for you?"

• "Although the timing for our meeting isn't urgent, the reason is. I will gladly meet with you on any day and time you select during the next 30 days."

---

129. Closing Tip

■ Never begin a second closing meeting with "Did you make a decision?" Instead, give yourself the opportunity to summarize key points.

---

131. Tip for Setting Ask Amount

■ **Gifts of real estate:** One rule of thumb for real estate gifts is to figure from 5 to 20 percent of total real estate property holdings. (One major university bases calculations on 9 percent of real estate holdings valued at below $400,000 and 25 percent of holdings valued at more than $600,000.)

---

132. Rules of Thumb

• While this rule has many exceptions, it generally takes from 18 to 24 months of active cultivation before a relationship with a prospect is mature enough to ask for a gift.

• One measure of a person's average net worth may be calculated to be 10 times the individual's annual salary (probably more realistic for salaries in excess of $100,000).

---

128. Advice on Face-to-face Calls

■ Never meet with a prospect or donor without first having identified the purpose of your visit. Each contact should, in some way, serve to move the individual closer to making a gift. (Even a thank-you call should move the donor closer to making a subsequent gift.)

List your call objective on each completed call report.

---

130. Be Up Front in Setting Solicitation Appointments

When setting an appointment that may result in a gift request, be up front in the purpose of your call. If the would-be donor is still willing to meet, your odds of securing a gift will go up. If however, the decision maker is unwilling to meet, you save time and can move on to more willing contacts. Here's an example of appointment-setting wording:

Development Officer: "I'm calling to set an appointment with you, and I promise not to take more than 30 minutes of your time. Is there a day and time that works for you?"

Decision Maker: "What is the purpose of your call?"

Development Officer: "I want to update you on how our agency is impacting the community and provide more detail on any aspects of our programs that may interest you, especially those that you may choose to support."

Once an appointment is set, send a confirmation letter restating your visit's purpose.

---

133. Offer Compelling Argument For Major Gifts Support

Need more ammunition for inviting major gift support? Add this powerful argument to your major gift solicitation repertoire:

"With the financial burdens currently facing the nation, you can be sure government funding for nonprofits will diminish. That's why support from the private sector is now more important than ever. Gifts from individuals and businesses and foundations were important during a thriving economy, but now it's critical if we are to maintain vital services."

134. Keep Testing New Calling Approaches

When calling on businesses for support, see if this approach sounds all too familiar: Establish rapport, make small talk, build the case for support then make the ask for an unrestricted gift to support general operations.

Instead of the same old, same old, why not vary your approach? In addition to being a lot less boring, doing so lets you test different presentation techniques and funding opportunities to see what works best.

Here's some of what you can test:

1. **Make team calls rather than making all calls alone.** Bring a board member along on some calls one day. Try asking your mayor to accompany you on some calls. Ask a respected CEO or someone served by your organization if she/he would accompany you on three calls.

2. **Say it differently.** Deliver your presentation in various ways to see what works best and to break up the monotony. Compare the prospect's business to your organization. Share a dream of what could be. Use story telling to build a compelling case for support.

3. **Try different props.** Rather than leaving behind the standard annual fund brochure, try something new. Share a handful of photos that help the prospect visualize the gift opportunity. Share a brief recording.

4. **Vary your funding projects.** In addition to unrestricted gifts, define specific projects that might interest

prospects more: sponsoring a particular program, enhancing a supplies budget, providing professional development funds for your employees, etc.

Emphasize Economic Impact

When approaching businesses to give to your annual fund, capital campaign or sponsor a special event, be clear about what's in it for them. Point out your organization's economic impact to the community, citing factors such as:

✓ Your organization's total budget and yearly payroll, pointing out the multiplier effect of those dollars in your community.

✓ Number of employees. If you represent a large organization, cite your ranking for number of employees: "We're the fifth largest employer in the city."

✓ The financial impact of your programs/services — savings to the community based on prevention programs, for example.

✓ Quality of life issues — cultural, athletic and educational opportunities for example.

✓ Business-oriented services — employee programs or discounts, for example.

135. Master a Handful Of Delivery Presentations

It's so easy to fall into a rut when meeting with prospective donors month after month, year after year. You've given that same spiel so many times that it becomes difficult to really concentrate of what you're saying.

To stay pumped for those important sales pitches, work at creating a handful of different deliveries from which you can choose — one that best fits the circumstances.

Spend a day creating outlines for four different presentations from which you can choose. Maybe your organization's community and economic impact will be the theme of one presentation. Perhaps anecdotes about those who have benefited from your services will be the theme of another.

Once you have developed the outlines, practice them with colleagues. Look for ways to make your presentations more compelling. Then test each of them as you meet with prospects to determine which works best.

136. Closing Techniques

- **Urgency Close** — This closing technique often involves a deadline: "For your gift to count toward the challenge, it will need to be received before June 30."

- **Leading Questions Close** — Ask the prospect processing questions that naturally lead toward a formal gift commitment: "Do you prefer that this scholarship be limited to women?" "Would you like your sponsorship to include your company logo on all signage?"

- **Conditional Close** — If the prospect offers an objection, make the gift a condition of resolving their objection:
  Prospect objection: "I'd better not commit myself. I have one year left on a pledge to the Y's capital campaign."
  Solicitor: "If your pledge to us spells out that payments won't begin for a year, would you feel better about making a commitment to our campaign now?"

- **The Either/Or Close** — This closing method makes the assumption that a gift is forthcoming and offers the giver a choice. For example: "Would you prefer to support our 2006 scholarship effort or to make a gift to the athletic program?"

137. Recognize What Gets Negotiated

Let's assume you have developed the proper relationship with a major gift prospect, know his/her interests, have framed your solicitation around those interests and have invited all key decision makers — spouse, attorney, children — to your solicitation meeting. At that point, you have three items to negotiate in getting a yes to a major gift:

1. **The size of the gift.** The size of the gift can be influenced by the other two negotiation items: payment method and period of payment.

2. **The method of payment.** Will the donor fund his/her gift with a cash, stock, real property or some combination of assets?

3. **The period of payment.** Will it be a one-time payment or given over a period of years? Will it include a planned gift provision?

Knowing what can be negotiated provides you with leverage in setting each of the above listed elements.

139. No Ask, No Gift

People make contributions when asked to do so. The only direct ways of asking include: a) face to face, b) phone, c) direct mail/e-mail. Whenever people in your development shop aren't taking one of those actions, they're not raising gifts.

140. Overcoming Rejection: Work at Improving Resiliency

All successful fundraisers experience rejection. It's the law of probability. But it's the ability to bounce back that separates the most successful development personnel from others.

How resilient are you? When a gift request is denied, work at diminishing any feelings of failure or other negative vibes. Here are three ways to do so:

1. **Recognize that external factors exist that can influence a person's decision to give:** other funding priorities, timing, financial constraints, personal issues, etc.

2. **Don't take failures too seriously.** Turn your mind to humor when those feelings of failure emerge. Recognize the true healing power of laughter.

3. **Know that rejection puts you one step closer to your next win.** If it takes five rejections, on average, before you realize a successful solicitation, each rejection is a step closer to that next triumph. See the rejection for what it is — a temporary bump in your road to success.

138. Create a Handout That Invites Endowment Gifts

If you're serious about building your endowment, it's important that you have at least one pamphlet or booklet that speaks to that issue.

Many nonprofits that already have named endowment funds will include the names of those funds and a brief description of each in their materials. Including descriptions of existing funds accomplishes two goals:

1. Existing endowment funds help would-be donors see that others have established named endowments and help to illustrate how the process works.

2. The brochure can be shared with donors whose names appear in it as an act of stewardship. These same donors may be inclined to add more to their endowed funds. Some nonprofits will even categorize named funds according to size as a subtle way to motivate adding to existing funds.

Endowment ABC's

Everything you need to know to make an endowment gift to ABC Charity

141. Prospect Conversation Starters

Instead of commenting on the weather, greet your donor prospect with a more significant conversation starter that shows you value the person, such as:

- Bringing in a photograph from a recent event or typical day at your agency that shows your clients using a recently funded piece of equipment, newly renovated facility or other benefit made possible by your generous donors.

- Making note of an accomplishment the individual and/or his/her business has made recently (e.g., being featured in the business section).

- Sharing a news clipping regarding a personal subject or hobby brought up by your prospect in an earlier visit (e.g., a travel article on a location he/she has visited or is planning to visit, or a magazine article on authentic Indian cooking).

142. Determine the Spouse's Role In Decision-making

Anyone who's been in the development profession for any length of time has probably came across an instance in which friction developed because one spouse was solicited for a gift without including the other spouse. That's why it's so important when approaching a married individual for a gift — particularly larger gifts — to be sensitive to both individuals' roles.

These phrases illustrate the solicitor's sensitivity to both spouses:

"I would welcome the opportunity to meet with both you and your wife if that can be arranged."

"I want to be sure to give you an opportunity to visit with your husband before making a final decision."

"If I could discuss this with both of you, it might help eliminate any questions as you consider your participation in our campaign."

143. Who Merits Face-to-face Calls?

How much thought do you put into who gets called on in person for a gift versus who gets contacted via phone, direct mail or e-mail?

To best manage your limited time, establish parameters to decide who you'll attempt to see on a face-to-face basis. While there will obviously be exceptions to the rule, calling guidelines will help prioritize who you most want to see. Some personal contact priorities, for example, could be based on all or some of the following criteria:

- Anyone who has given or has the potential of giving $500 or more annually.

- All current and former board members.

- Any businesses/individuals who sponsored or could sponsor programs/projects.

- All foundations that have provided grants in recent years or have the potential of providing grants.

- All pre-qualified planned gift prospects.

144. Give 'Ben Franklin Close' a Try

The same sage who gave American society wise words such as "a penny saved is a penny earned" and "time is money" is also credited with a closing technique: The Ben Franklin Close.

This closing method involves listing the pros and cons of making a gift to your charity.

Wondering how this method earned its Ben Franklin label? Rumor has it that when wise Ben Franklin was trying to make up his mind about something, he'd write the pros and cons on either side of a sheet of paper. An example of how to put Franklin's method to use in swaying a gift prospect your way is shown below.

Pluses	Minuses
Helps those in need Makes our charity stronger Helps our community Gets membership in Gold Leaf Society Tax-deductible	Requires financial sacrifice

145. How to React When a Prospect Says No

You made the request for a specific amount and sat back and patiently waited for the prospect to reply. She responded with a plain-and-simple no. What now? Do you:

A. Politely thank the prospect for her time and leave?

B. Ask again, only for a lesser amount?

C. Attempt to find out the rationale behind the no?

D. All of the above?

In most cases, you might attempt all of the above (D), but not necessarily in that order. Experience is the best teacher for determining if a refusal to give might be based on timing, nature of the request, amount of the request or a combination of factors. Always thank the prospect for having considered a gift, and attempt to understand the rationale for declining your request. Equally important, do what is possible to keep the door open for a future invitation to invest in your mission.

146. Closing Technique

1-2-3 Close — With this gift closing technique, the solicitor points out three reasons for making the suggested gift amount. The technique — the principle of triples where three reasons are given together — acts as a compelling message that adds legitimacy and urgency to the request. Here's an example:

"By making a $1,000 now, you will:

1. Help us meet this year's challenging annual fund goal,

2. Become a member of the exclusive Order of St. James gift club, and

3. Do more than you can imagine to help those we serve."

147. Position Your Frame of Mind

What are your thoughts just prior to making a prospect call? If you're like most people, thoughts of possible rejection may be going through your mind — especially if you feel the least bit intimated by the person on whom you're calling. But you can change that.

As you near the point of meeting with a prospect, make a conscious effort to switch your mental gears. Rather than thinking "rejection, intimidation, objections, etc.," think opportunity: "Here's an opportunity for me to tell this deserving person about the important mission of our organization! Here's an opportunity for me to invite this person to become more closely associated with the rewards of our work! Here's this person's opportunity to invest!"

That conscious effort to readjust your thinking prior to a call will result in an energizing experience for both you and the individual who is about to make a donation.

148. Empathize With Prospects Who Voice Objections

You've spent months cultivating a prospect and it's time to pop the question. But as you're about to ask for a gift, the prospect interrupts with, "You folks should be paying more attention to what's going on right here in our town!"

How do you respond to this or other type of objection by a prospect?

With immediate empathy. Stop what you're doing or saying, immediately switch gears and listen — empathetically. Give the person your undivided attention. Put yourself in the shoes of the prospect. See the issue like he/she sees it. Often, listening to someone's objection is half the battle in resolving it.

After listening, maybe even rephrasing the objection back to the person so he or she knows you fully understand it, assure the prospect you will give his/her concern some level of attention, e.g.: "I'm going to share this with the executive director and get back to you."

Only after fully addressing the person's concern should you decide whether to return to the solicitation or wait for a more appropriate time.

149. Recruit, Manage a Major Gifts Advisory Committee

Just because your development office is small doesn't mean you can't raise big gifts.

Follow these steps to create a volunteer-driven major gifts advisory committee that will expand your efforts in identifying, researching, cultivating and soliciting significant gifts:

1. Begin by developing a written job description for your group and presenting it to your board for approval. It's important to get board buy-in for your major gifts program. In fact, include board representation on your committee.

2. Recruit a small group — say five to eight individuals who have either made a significant gift to your charity or have the ability to make a major gift — to serve a one- or two-year term on the committee. Look for those with connections to wealth.

3. Meet for up to two hours a month to begin a system of: building a manageable list of major gift prospects, prioritizing prospects based on financial capability and proclivity to give, developing individual cultivation plans for each, determining who should meet with whom, and knowing assignments for the month ahead.

4. Develop a printed description of five or six gift opportunities for you and the advisory committee to share with prospects as cultivation becomes more intense and focused.

5. Use subsequent meetings to report progress and decide on next steps.